W9-CIA-381

COMPUTERS, INTERNET, AND SOCIETY

Computer Ethics

COMPUTERS, INTERNET, AND SOCIETY

Computer Ethics

Robert Plotkin

Facts On File
An Infobase Learning Company

SOMERSET CO. LIBRARY
BRIDGEWATER, N.J. 08807

COMPUTER ETHICS

Copyright © 2012 by Robert Plotkin

All rights reserved. No part of this book may be reproduced or utilized in any form or by any means, electronic or mechanical, including photocopying, recording, or by any information storage or retrieval systems, without permission in writing from the publisher. For information contact:

Facts On File
An imprint of Infobase Learning
132 West 31st Street
New York NY 10001

Library of Congress Cataloging-in-Publication Data

Plotkin, Robert, 1971–
  Computer ethics / Robert Plotkin.
      p. cm. — (Computers, internet, and society)
  Includes bibliographical references and index.
  ISBN 978-0-8160-7755-7
  1. Electronic data processing—Moral and ethical aspects. I. Title.
  QA76.9.M65P46 2011
  004—dc22   2010050907

Facts On File books are available at special discounts when purchased in bulk quantities for businesses, associations, institutions, or sales promotions. Please call our Special Sales Department in New York at (212) 967-8800 or (800) 322-8755.

You can find Facts On File on the World Wide Web at http://www.infobaselearning.com

Excerpts included herewith have been reprinted by permission of the copyright holders; the author has made every effort to contact copyright holders. The publishers will be glad to rectify, in future editions, any errors or omissions brought to their notice.

Text design by Kerry Casey
Composition by Hermitage Publishing Services
Illustrations by Bobbi McCutcheon
Photo research by Suzanne M. Tibor
Cover printed by Bang Printing, Brainerd, Minn.
Book printed and bound by Bang Printing, Brainerd, Minn.
Date printed: October 2011
Printed in the United States of America

10 9 8 7 6 5 4 3 2 1

This book is printed on acid-free paper.

CONTENTS

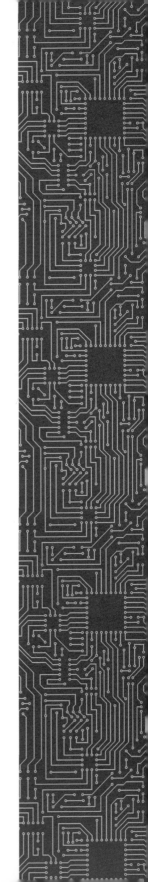

PREFACE

Computers permeate innumerable aspects of people's lives. For example, computers are used to communicate with friends and family, analyze finances, play games, watch movies, listen to music, purchase products and services, and learn about the world. People increasingly use computers without even knowing it, as microprocessors containing software replace mechanical and electrical components in everything from automobiles to microwave ovens to wristwatches.

Conversations about computers tend to focus on their technological features, such as how many billions of calculations they can perform per second, how much memory they contain, or how small they have become. We have good reason to be amazed at advances in computer technology over the last 50 years. According to one common formulation of Moore's law (named after Gordon Moore of Intel Corporation), the number of transistors on a chip doubles roughly every two years. As a result, a computer that can be bought for $1,000 today is as powerful as a computer that cost more than $1 million just 15 years ago.

Although such technological wonders are impressive in their own right, we care about them not because of the engineering achievements they represent but because they have changed how people interact every day. E-mail not only enables communication with existing friends and family more quickly and less expensively but also lets us forge friendships with strangers halfway across the globe. Social networking platforms such as Twitter and Facebook enable nearly instant, effortless communication among large groups of people without requiring the time or effort needed to compose and read e-mail messages. These and other forms of communication are facilitated by increasingly powerful mobile handheld devices, such as the BlackBerry and iPhone, which make it possible for people to communicate at any time and in any place, thereby eliminating the need for a desktop computer with a hardwired Internet connection. Such improvements in technology have led to changes in society, often in complex and unexpected ways.

Understanding the full impact that computers have on society therefore requires an appreciation of not only what computers can do but also how computer technology is used in practice and its effects on human behavior and attitudes.

Computers, Internet, and Society is a timely multivolume set that seeks to provide students with such an understanding. The set includes the following six titles, each of which focuses on a particular context in which computers have a significant social impact:

- *Communication and Cyberspace*
- *Computer Ethics*
- *Computers and Creativity*
- *Computers in Science and Mathematics*
- *Computers in the Workplace*
- *Privacy, Security, and Cyberspace*

It is the goal of each volume to accomplish the following:

- explain the history of the relevant computer technology, what such technology can do today, and how it works;
- explain how computers interact with human behavior in a particular social context; and
- encourage readers to develop socially responsible attitudes and behaviors in their roles as computer users and future developers of computer technology.

New technology can be so engrossing that people often adopt it—and adapt their behavior to it—quickly and without much forethought. Yesterday's students gathered in the schoolyard to plan for a weekend party; today they meet online on a social networking Web site. People flock to such new features as soon as they come available, as evidenced by the long lines at the store every time a newer, smarter phone is announced.

Most such developments are positive. Yet they also carry implications for our *privacy,* freedom of speech, and *security,* all of which are easily overlooked if one does not pause to think about them. The paradox of today's computer technology is that it is both everywhere and invisible. The goal of this set is to make such technology visible so that it, and its impact on society, can be examined, as well as to assist students in using conceptual tools for making informed and responsible decisions about how to both apply and further develop that technology now and as adults.

Although today's students are more computer savvy than all of the generations that preceded them, many students are more familiar with what computers can do than with how computers work or the social changes being wrought by computers. Students who use the Internet constantly may remain unaware of how computers can be used to invade their privacy or steal their identity or how journalists and human rights activists use computer encryption technology to keep their communications secret and secure from oppressive governments around the world. Students who have grown up copying information from the World Wide Web and downloading songs, videos, and feature-length films onto computers, iPods, and cell phones may not understand the circumstances under which those activities are legitimate and when they violate copyright law. And students who have only learned about scientists and inventors in history books probably are unaware that today's innovators are using computers to discover new drugs and write pop music at the touch of a button.

In fact, young people have had such close and ongoing interactions with computers since they were born that they often lack the historical perspective to understand just how much computers have made their lives different from those of their parents. Computers form as much of the background of students' lives as the air they breathe; as a result, they tend to take both for granted. This set, therefore, is highly relevant and important to students because it enables them to understand not only how computers work but also how computer technology has affected their lives. The goal of this set is to provide students with the intellectual tools needed to think critically about computer technology so that they can make informed and responsible decisions about how to both use and further develop that technology now and as adults.

This set reflects my long-standing personal and professional interest in the intersection between computer technology, law, and society. I started programming computers when I was about 10 years old and my fascination with the technology has endured ever since. I had the honor of studying computer science and engineering at the Massachusetts Institute of Technology (MIT) and then studying law at the Boston University School of Law, where I now teach a course entitled, "Software and the Law." Although I spend most of my time as a practicing patent lawyer, focusing on patent protection for computer technology, I have also spoken and written internationally on topics including patent protection for software, freedom of speech, electronic privacy, and ethical implications of releasing potentially harmful software. My book, *The Genie in the Machine,* explores the impact of computer-automated inventing on law, businesses, inventors, and consumers.

What has been most interesting to me has been to study not any one aspect of computer technology, but rather to delve into the wide range of ways in which such technology affects, and is affected by, society. As a result, a multidisciplinary set such as this is a perfect fit for my background and interests. Although it can be challenging to educate non-technologists about how computers work, I have written and spoken about such topics to audiences including practicing lawyers, law professors, computer scientists and engineers, ethicists, philosophers, and historians. Even the work that I have targeted solely to lawyers has been multidisciplinary in nature, drawing on the history and philosophy of computer technology to provide context and inform my legal analysis. I specifically designed my course on "Software and the Law" to be understandable to law students with no background in computer technology. I have leveraged this experience in explaining complex technical concepts to lay audiences in the writing of this multidisciplinary set for a student audience in a manner that is understandable and engaging to students of any background.

The world of computers changes so rapidly that it can be difficult even for those of us who spend most of our waking hours learning about the latest developments in computer technology to stay up to date. The term *technological singularity* has even been coined to refer to a point, perhaps not too far in the future, when the rate of technological change will become so rapid that essentially no time elapses between one technological advance and the next. For better or worse, time does elapse between writing a series of books such as this and the date of publication. With full awareness of the need to provide students with current and relevant information, every effort has been made, up to the time at which these volumes are shipped to the printers, to ensure that each title in this set is as up to date as possible.

ACKNOWLEDGMENTS

Many people deserve thanks for making this series a reality. First, my thanks to my literary agent, Jodie Rhodes, for introducing me to Facts On File. When she first approached me, it was to ask whether I knew any authors who were interested in writing a set of books on a topic that I know nothing about—I believe it was biology. In response, I asked whether there might be interest in a topic closer to my heart—computers and society—and, as they say, the rest is history.

Frank Darmstadt, my editor, has not only held my hand through all of the high-level planning and low-level details involved in writing a series of this magnitude but also exhibited near superhuman patience in the face of drafts whose separation in time could be marked by the passing of the seasons. He also helped me to toe the fine dividing line between the forest and the trees and between today's technological marvels and tomorrow's long-forgotten fads—a distinction that is particularly difficult to draw in the face of rapidly changing technology. I also thank Michael Axon for his incisive review of the manuscript and Alexandra Simon for her superb copyediting.

Several research assistants, including Catie Watson, Rebekah Judson, Jessica McElrath, and Sue Keeler, provided invaluable aid in uncovering and summarizing information about technologies ranging from the ancient to the latest gadgets we carry in our pockets. In particular, Luba Jabsky performed extensive research that formed the foundation of many of the book's chapters and biographies.

The artwork and photographs have brought the text to life. Although computer science, with its microscopic electronic components and abstract software modules, is a particularly difficult field to illustrate, line artist Bobbi McCutcheon and photo researcher Suzie Tibor could not have matched visuals to text more perfectly.

Last, but not least, I thank my family, including my partner, Melissa, and my dog, Maggie, for standing by my side and at my feet, respectively, as I spent my evenings and weekends trying, through words and pictures, to convey to the next generation some of the wonder and excitement in computer technology that I felt as a teenager.

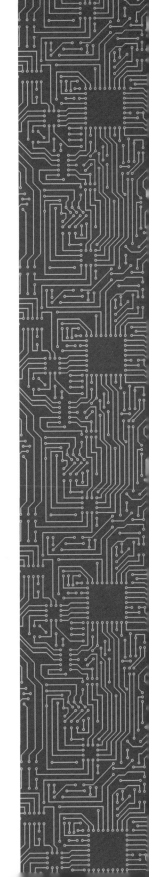

INTRODUCTION

Computers can be used to cause many kinds of harm, and every such use raises ethical questions. For example, computers can be used to spread *viruses*, which can be used to invade the privacy of others, steal financial information and other data, destroy information, and even cause physical harm—such as by shutting down a power plant. Many *white hat hackers* claim that not only are they justified in spreading viruses, but that doing so is socially beneficial because it alerts the public to security vulnerabilities in existing computer technology, thereby prodding the manufacturers of those technologies to plug their security holes and stay on their feet more generally. This debate over the relative merits and demerits of spreading viruses or, in a weaker form, publishing information about *computer security* vulnerabilities, continues to rage among computer security experts.

Even those of us who merely use rather than develop computer technology face ethical quandaries. Does the easy accessibility of written works, music, videos, and other content on the Internet make it ethically permissible to access, copy, and redistribute that content? Is it ethically permissible to look at someone else's documents on a home or school computer just because they are not protected by password? Are there any ethical problems with using a false identity in an Internet chat room or behaving in that chat room in a way in which one would not consider acting in the real world? What about using a photograph from the Internet in a research paper without giving credit to the photographer, even if using that photo constitutes *fair use* and therefore does not violate the law? *Computer Ethics* explores questions such as these to enable students to understand the need to think about the difference between what is lawful and what is ethical in the context of computers and the Internet.

In particular, chapter 1 examines the ways in which computers have made it easier to invade the privacy of others, both intentionally and unintentionally. It begins by discussing the nature of privacy, including how privacy was viewed before technology became a major force in society. Some of the negative consequences that can result from the *anonymity* of the Internet are described, such as the ease of assuming a false identity and the dangers of *cyberbullying* and *cyberharassment*. The impact of cyberbullying and cyberharassment is illustrated by some tragic recent cases. The efforts to discourage this destructive behavior and prosecute those who engage in it are discussed. This chapter also describes the work of academics defining the changing ethics related to privacy for our digital age. One of the most controversial areas of *computer ethics* involves the role of online privacy in the workplace. This chapter discusses the rights of both employer and employee in relation to computer privacy. Employers often require employees to keep company information private, but what about illegal or unethical information? *Whistle-blowers* are employees who decide that exposing their employer's wrongdoing is the ethical thing to do. This chapter describes some famous whistle-blower cases, including that of the employee who exposed fraud at Enron Corporation. Chapter 1 concludes with an exploration of the ethical issues involved with retaining and destroying computer data.

Chapter 2 explores ethical issues related to computer security. It begins by focusing on computer viruses and other forms of malicious software. A brief explanation of how viruses, worms, and *phishing* schemes work is provided, along with information about some of the most famous cases of malicious software. The security mechanisms used to protect individual computers are described, including *password protection,* data encryption, and *antivirus software.* The chapter then examines how the increased use of the Internet and computer networks has led to the need for more sophisticated security mechanisms for large-scale computer systems used by businesses, financial institutions, and government agencies. Flaws in the design and implementation of computer software, also referred to as *bugs,* are another source of security problems in computers. Ethical questions related to software bugs are addressed in this chapter, including whether software companies should go public with information about known software security bugs.

Chapter 3 examines the pros and cons of the anonymous communication that is enabled by computers. Case studies related to the use of anonymous online identities are presented. The role of the whistle-blower is again examined, this time in relation to whether or not a whistle-blower should be allowed to remain anonymous. Some notable cases of both anonymous and non-anonymous whistle-blowers are presented. The focus then moves to anonymous news sources and the ethical responsibilities of journalists who use anonymous sources. *WikiLeaks,* a nonprofit media organization, accepts anonymous information, which, after being verified and analyzed, is published. The chapter concludes with a description of some of the mechanisms used by computers to differentiate between legitimate users of an application and anonymous spammers.

Chapter 4 explores the simulated computer environments known as virtual worlds. What began as text-based systems that required large doses of user imagination have evolved into online multiplayer games like World of Warcraft and simulated versions of reality like The Sims and *Second Life*. The technology behind today's virtual world software is described and a history of the Second Life application is provided. The chapter concludes with an examination of the complex ethical questions related to simulated environments, including a description of a simulated crime that took place in an early virtual world. A form of cyberbullying known as *griefing*, which involves antisocial behavior in online games and virtual worlds, is also discussed.

Chapter 5 returns to the subject of software bugs, explaining how and why bugs are introduced into software by programmers. The difficulties in producing bug-free software are discussed and the ethics of releasing software with known bugs is explored. To illustrate the potential danger of software bugs, some cases of bugs that have caused catastrophic damages and loss of life are described. This examination of software bugs also looks at the role that programmers' ethical values play and considers whether the ultimate blame for bugs lies with the individual programmer or with the programmer's employer. The chapter concludes by describing efforts to establish a standard *code of ethics* for computer professionals.

Chapter 6 focuses on the ethics of copying computer data. The sheer volume of information now available on the Internet and the ease of copying it have increased the temptation for *plagiarism* of written material. As seen in the plagiarism case of the *New York Times* journalist Jayson Blair, professional writers are not immune from the urge to copy the work of others. Even authors who do not intend to plagiarize may do so by failing to provide attribution when using the work of others. This chapter considers the lengths to which some academic institutions have gone to detect plagiarism on the part of students. The legal concepts of copyright, fair use, and the *public domain* are described, and some illustrative examples are provided. Over the past few years, the royalty-free sharing of MP3 music files has tested the power of copyright law in the digital age. This chapter concludes with a description of the action taken by the Recording Industry Association of America (RIAA) against Napster and other file-sharing services.

Chapter 7 examines the ways in which the Internet is shaping human communication. The immediacy, reach, and permanency of online information means that opinions posted on the Internet can have far-reaching and long-lasting impacts. Social networks, blogs, forums, and chat rooms give the average person with an Internet connection the power to create content that may be read and copied by anyone in the world. This chapter explores how the use of the Internet as a tool of free speech has raised ethical and legal questions that have yet to be answered. Some landmark cases that have pushed the limits of offensive and explicit speech on the Internet are described, as well as attempts to censor or filter Internet content. Finally, this chapter discusses the ethics involved in posting publicly available information that may be damaging to an individual or to the public good.

Chapter 8 focuses on the rules and conventions for good online manners, also known as *netiquette*. The informal nature of written content in e-mail, instant messages, and tweets has dispensed with many traditional rules of etiquette related to written communications. A set of netiquette guidelines that was originally described in 1995 by an engineer named Sally Hambridge is still timely and is discussed in this chapter. New conventions that have evolved for computer communications are described, including the use of *emoticons* (or *smileys*) to convey emotions. This chapter concludes with a description of the history and meaning of emoticons and acronyms, or initialisms, such as LOL and TMI.

PRIVACY: DOES IT EXIST ONLINE?

In 1890, in an academic paper entitled "The Right to Privacy," Samuel D. Warren and Louis D. Brandeis (a justice of the U.S. Supreme Court from 1916–39) argued the following:

> Recent inventions and business methods call attention to the next step which must be taken for the protection of the person, and for securing to the individual what Judge Cooley calls the right "to be let alone." Instantaneous photographs and newspaper enterprise have invaded the sacred precincts of private and domestic life; and numerous mechanical devices threaten to make good the prediction that "what is whispered in the closet shall be proclaimed from the house-tops."

In short, Warren and Brandeis claimed that new communications technology necessitated the recognition of a new legal right to privacy. A century later, Sun Microsystems CEO Scott McNealy proclaimed: "Privacy is dead. Get over it." It is no accident that Mr. McNealy was an executive of a technology firm. Rather, his view that the increasingly widespread availability of technology that is capable of disseminating private information inevitably will—and possibly should—lead to the elimination of privacy is common among technologists. Just as persistent, however, is Warren and Brandeis's contrary view that the existence of privacy-breaching technology is cause for strengthening privacy rights, not abandoning them. This chapter explores the ongoing tension between these competing positions and the ways in which they continue to play out in the digital and online worlds.

THE STRUGGLE TO MAINTAIN PRIVACY IN THE DIGITAL WORLD

Before the advent of computers, one could reasonably expect to maintain the privacy of sensitive information—such as medical records, wills, and diaries—by locking it in a safe or by keeping it in one's home and showing it only to family members and trusted friends. In such circumstances, it was relatively clear that taking such documents from someone's home without permission and revealing the information they contained to the public constituted unethical behavior. Furthermore, the amount of forethought and effort required to reveal such information—such as planning to break into a safe, then breaking into it, taking documents from it, and sending the documents to a newspaper—meant that few except those who were intent on engaging in unethical behavior would follow through to the end.

Yet today computers and the Internet are making it increasingly easy to reveal private or otherwise sensitive information about other people in ways that can lead to embarrassment or worse. Such acts may even be undertaken unintentionally, such as by mistakenly forwarding personal photographs to a large group of people by hitting the Reply All button instead of to a single close friend by hitting the Reply button. This increased ease with which it is becoming possible to violate the privacy of others raises new questions about what constitutes ethical and unethical conduct in relation to privacy. For example, consider just the following small sampling of online activities and ask whether they are ethical or unethical:

- using someone else's password, without that person's permission, to access files on that person's computer;
- logging in to someone else's e-mail account using that person's password, without permission, and sending e-mail messages under that person's name;
- logging in to someone else's e-mail account using that person's password, with that person's permission, and sending e-mail messages under that person's name without making your true identity clear to the recipients of the e-mail messages you send;
- viewing Web pages, blog postings, or postings on social networks that someone else clearly intended to keep private but unintentionally made public;

- selling a list of customers of an e-commerce Web site to advertisers to use in sending targeted advertising to the customers; and
- reading e-mail messages on the computer of a person who walked away from a computer without locking the screen.

If the ease with which any of these actions can be performed makes it tempting to conclude that the action is ethical rather than unethical, then how does any of these actions differ from breaking into a safe and taking private documents from it, other than by the ease of engaging in the former activity over the latter? This chapter examines such questions and, more generally, how to make responsible personal decisions about ethical uses of computer technology in relation to privacy.

The goal of this examination of computers, the Internet, and ethics is not to imply that any action that might possibly reveal the private information of another person is always and absolutely unethical. Not only is total privacy impossible; in some situations it is permissible to reveal information about other people without their permission. A clear example is private information about a politician that reflects on his ability to serve the public. For example, it would not be unethical for a reporter to publish a newspaper article revealing that a state governor who has campaigned for fiscal responsibility in government has failed to file his own personal tax returns for several years. In fact, a reporter who uncovers such information might have an ethical duty to reveal such information to the public. Yet it may be unethical for a reporter to reveal the same kind of information about a private individual, such as a bus driver or a student, because there is no pressing need for the public to know about the private financial affairs of such people. As this simple example demonstrates, whether a particular action is ethical or unethical can vary depending on the circumstances. Because the rapid development of computer technology is constantly changing the circumstances in which private information is handled, it can be difficult to draw clear conclusions about whether revealing such information in particular circumstances is ethical or not.

Another way to understand why revealing personal information about someone else without that person's permission may not necessarily constitute a breach of privacy is that every person comes to expect only a certain degree of privacy in social interactions with others and therefore does not consider all access by other people to their private information to constitute a breach of trust.

These expectations, however, vary from relationship to relationship and from situation to situation. For example, most people reasonably expect nearly complete privacy within their own homes, particularly if they have not invited anyone else inside. As a result, standing outside someone's home and taking pictures of that person through a window is considered unethical in almost any circumstance. Yet taking a picture of a cashier through the window of a retail clothing store on a busy street is most likely not unethical because people who work in such stores expect to be observed by many people throughout the course of the day. Expectations of privacy vary from situation to situation, and actions that constitute violations of privacy are those that violate others' reasonable expectations of privacy.

Streets in many major cities are monitored continuously by surveillance cameras, not all of which are visible to pedestrians. In this photo, an Operations Center Crime Surveillance Specialist monitors screens displaying views from cameras located on the streets of Chicago at the Chicago Emergency Communications Center in an attempt to detect signs of actual or potential crimes. *(Joshua Lott/Reuters/Landov)*

It can be difficult to determine, however, exactly what is reasonable for someone to expect in the context of privacy. Twenty years ago, it might have been reasonable for someone walking down an isolated street late at night to assume that his or her activities were not being observed or at least not being recorded on videotape. In such circumstances, using a video camera from a rooftop to record someone walking down a street might have been considered an unethical breach of the pedestrian's privacy. Now, however, many city streets are lined with *surveillance cameras,* often so small and well placed that they remain hidden to all but those who look carefully for them. For example, London, England, has extensively adopted *closed circuit television (CCTV) cameras* for the purpose of detecting and investigating crimes, with one estimate concluding that there are around 1.5 million cameras in city centers, stations, airports, retail stores, and other public places in London. Whether or not such cameras are effective at achieving their intended goal, they raise the question whether such widespread placement of cameras should lead the population generally to lower its expectation of privacy in public spaces. This leads, in turn, to the question whether the adoption of additional surveillance measures in public places should now be considered ethical because members of the public no longer expect that any of their actions in public will remain private in any way. Yet if this conclusion is correct, it is arguably based on circular logic, namely that putting technology into place for violating people's privacy leads them to expect less and less privacy, as a result of which the technology no longer violates people's privacy because it does not upset people's lowered privacy expectations. Thus, the development and adoption of new technology that is capable of capturing and disseminating personal information about individuals can lead to a downward privacy spiral from which there is no return, at least if the *reasonable expectation of privacy* is the yardstick against which all privacy violations are measured.

One way to attempt to resolve this dilemma is to look at the history of privacy in the context of older technologies. Before computers were used to create, organize, and store information, information was spoken or stored on paper. Therefore, one way to determine whether a particular use of someone else's personal information constitutes an unethical breach of privacy is to ask whether such an action would have been unethical if it had been performed in the precomputer, paper-based world. This way of thinking views technology as just a change in form not substance, thereby allowing one to apply preexisting moral precepts to it and to escape from the conclusion that any transmission of information is ethical simply because computers now make it possible. Under such analysis, reading someone else's private journal on a computer that had accidentally been left unlocked would be unethical, because reading a paper version of the journal after taking it from a mistakenly unlocked desk drawer would have been wrong.

As satisfying, and relieving, as it may feel to rely on old notions of ethics to resolve today's questions about electronic privacy, such an approach has limitations. For example, some situations that exist today have no equivalent in the precomputer world. It is difficult, for example, to find a real world analogy to the ongoing discussions that take place on social networking sites. Instead, such conversations seem to resemble a combination of several different kinds of real world communications, such as face-to-face conversations, public speeches given to a large audience, and newspaper articles. Like a face-to-face conversation, social networking messages can be transmitted from one person directly to another, but like a speech, they can sometimes be read by large numbers of additional people, and like a newspaper article they can be read long after they were first written. As a result, it is not possible to apply ethical conclusions from a single, preexisting type of real world communication to instant messages, postings on a Facebook wall, or Twitter tweets. Therefore, it is necessary to develop new ways to think about ethical behavior online, although old conclusions and logic can be extremely useful as a guide.

Consider a story that made the rounds of Web sites and blogs in late 2009. A teenage boy named Chris, who was punished after his sister Katie told his parents that he was hiding beer in his room, used Facebook to exact revenge on her. He searched his sister's bedroom and found her hook-up list written on a piece of paper, which he then scanned and published in electronic form on his Facebook page. The handwritten list contained the names of boys in Katie's school and descriptions of what Katie had done or wanted to do with each boy. The list itself, and the ensuing Facebook dialogue between Chris and Katie ("TAKE THIS DOWN NOW! WHAT THE **** IS WRONG WITH YOU?!?!?!"), quickly went viral. Whether the story is true or a well-executed hoax, it illustrates the privacy issues that are played out thousands of times a day on the Internet. In particular, it serves as a pointed example of the ways in which the relatively limited effects that such a juvenile taunt would have had in the precomputer days, when

(continues on page 8)

1001110100101010100110010111011010100101001

Cyberbullying and Cyberharassment

Bullies were the bane of shy and unpopular schoolchildren long before computers existed. Many adults who were bullied as children still remember being afraid to go to school because of the taunts they would have to suffer in the classroom, schoolyard, or gym class. However, before computers and the Internet, those who were the victims of bullies could at least escape the *harassment* at the end of the school day by going home or to the homes of their true friends.

Unfortunately, and sometimes tragically, the advent and widespread adoption of cell phones and Internet-connected computers by students have made it increasingly difficult to escape bullying. Of course, such technology has a beneficial side. Cell phones and computers have expanded the social circle of children and teenagers. Besides interacting with friends and acquaintances in person, they can also use instant messaging (IM), texting, and social networking Web sites to keep in touch with each other even when they cannot physically be together. Yet one of the most serious problems that young people encounter when they communicate electronically is online bullying, also known as cyberbullying. According to the National Crime Prevention Council, a nonprofit educational organization, almost half of American children and teenagers have been affected by cyberbullying.

The National Crime Prevention Council defines cyberbullying as the use of the Internet, a cell phone, or any electronic device "to send or post information or images meant to hurt or embarrass others." Cyberbullying can take a variety of forms. Threats, hate speech, sexual comments, and lies can be sent as messages or posted on Web sites or in online forums. Embarrassing photos and videos may be uploaded to a personal or public Web site. Cyberbullying also involves stealing someone else's log-in information and then publishing information using the other person's online identity with the purpose of harassing or ridiculing them.

Both boys and girls engage in cyberbullying, and both boys and girls are the victims of it. It can begin in early grade school and continue through high school and into college. It is often anonymous, with the perpetrators using temporary e-mail accounts, pseudonyms, and *avatars* to conceal their identities. This anonymity enables many cyberbullies to feel comfortable ignoring normal social constraints and to be bolder about engaging in cyberbullying without fear of

(continues)

1001110100101010100110010111011010100101001

(continued)

detection or punishment. Because the impact of cyberbullying is far-reaching and long lasting, it can have serious consequences. Victims of cyberbullying often experience a loss of self-esteem, as well as a variety of other emotional responses, including fear, anger, and frustration. Teenagers have killed themselves or others after being victimized by cyberbullying.

For example, in 2003, a 13-year-old teenager from Vermont named Ryan Halligan was the victim of both face-to-face bullying and cyberbullying. Classmates from Ryan's middle school sent IMs that threatened him and accused him of being gay. A girl who Ryan had a crush on pretended to like him, then used personal information to taunt him online. When Ryan confided online to another boy that he was considering suicide, the boy replied, "It's about time." One night in October 2003, while his family slept, Ryan ended his life by hanging himself in the bathroom of his home.

The term *cyberbullying* is used when all the parties involved are minors. When adults engage in this behavior, the terms cyberharassment and cyberstalking are applied. One of the most infamous examples of cyberharassment is the case of 13-year-old Megan Meier. In September 2006, Lori Drew, the mother of one of Megan's former friends, created a false identity on the Myspace social networking Web site. Impersonating a fictitious 13-year-old boy named Josh Evans, she manipulated and harassed Megan. As a result of her communication with "Josh Evans," Megan committed suicide in October 2006. The case became the first instance of the federal government using the Computer Fraud and Abuse Act (CFAA) to prosecute a violation on a social networking site. Lori Drew was found guilty of a misdemeanor violation of the CFAA in 2008 but was later acquitted on appeal.

Another case involving cyberharassment, video voyeurism, and social networking took place in September 2010. A 19-year-old Rutgers University student named Tyler Clementi was unknowingly filmed during an intimate encounter with

(continued from page 6)

Chris might have passed his sister's list around the cafeteria table to a handful of friends, can be multiplied by computers and the Internet that made it possible for the same information to reach thousands, if not millions, of people around the world. This raises the question whether actions that may have been annoying

`1001110100101010100110010111011010100101001`

another man in his dorm room. His dorm roommate, Dharun Ravi, watched the encounter on a webcam and posted information about it on Twitter. Three days later, after Ravi again posted information about Clementi on Twitter, Clementi committed suicide by jumping off the George Washington Bridge. He left a post on his Facebook page that said, "jumping off the gw bridge sorry." Eighteen-year-olds Dharun Ravi and Molly Wei were subsequently arrested, and Ravi was indicted on bias intimidation, invasion of privacy, witness intimidation, and other charges. His criminal case is still pending as of this writing.

Because cyberbullying and cyberharassment are relatively new offenses, it has been difficult to prosecute offenders. Schools have been sued for punishing children who engaged in cyberbullying off campus. In response, most states have amended or are in the processes of amending existing laws and policies related to school bullying to also include cyberbullying. At the federal level, the Megan Meier Cyberbullying Prevention Act (H.R. 1966) was introduced in 2009 and is still working its way through Congress. This act would criminalize the use of electronic communication to intimidate or harass another person. However, many people oppose H.R. 1966 on the grounds that it limits free speech.

In addition to the enactment of laws, one of the most effective weapons against cyberbullying is education. Parents and educators need to learn the signs of cyber-bullying and to be supportive of children and teenagers who are targeted. The National Crime Prevention Council encourages children and teenagers to help prevent cyberbullying by discouraging friends who cyberbully and refusing to pass on cyberbullying messages. A trusted adult should be notified when cyberbullying occurs. Furthermore, online and offline support groups are springing up to help victims of cyberbullying by giving them ways to cope, fight back, and understand that this time in their life will pass. Perhaps the best advice to any young person who is considering saying something online that might be hurtful to a peer is summed up by the phrase, "If you wouldn't say it in person, don't say it online."

`1001110100101010100110010111011010100101001`

but relatively harmless in the past can now become serious ethical infractions as the result of using computer technology to amplify the pain they cause.

The fields of electronic privacy and computer ethics are relatively new and continuously developing as technology itself develops. Ethical views of right and wrong in particular situations are perpetually playing catch-up to technological advances. Even in less rapidly changing times, people disagree sharply about ethics as a result of differences in religion, culture, and personal attitudes. Adding technology to the mix makes it that much more difficult to agree about what constitutes ethical behavior. As a result, neither this chapter nor this volume attempts to announce hard and fast rules about whether particular actions constitute violations of privacy or ethical behavior more generally. Instead, the focus is on how computer technology changes and broadens the ways in which people can and do interact, such as by making information more easily available and simpler to distribute. It is this very same quality that both makes computers unparalleled tools for communication and creates unforetold ways in which computers can be used to invade privacy. As more information about individuals becomes easily available to others, the field of computer ethics is concerned with the effect that such availability has on the meaning of privacy and on the obligations of others to refrain from accessing such information. The remainder of this chapter will explore these and other effects of computers and the Internet on privacy.

COMPUTERS, THE INTERNET, AND IDENTITY CRIMES

While the growth of computer technology has certainly increased the public's awareness of *identity theft,* impersonation is nothing new. Shakespeare wrote a whole catalogue of plays that hinge on impersonation. The con man was a staple of American culture long before Internet phishing schemes became prominent. Furthermore, techniques such as forging someone's signature or disguising a voice on the telephone are hardly recent innovations.

Computers and the Internet, however, make it easier than ever to impersonate someone. A famous 1993 *New Yorker* cartoon featured a dog sitting in front of a computer, his head turned toward a fellow canine, while underneath were written the words, "On the Internet, nobody knows you're a dog." While humorous, this statement also points out an important feature of Internet technology and culture: true and easy anonymity. Although every e-mail message carries the e-mail address of its sender, such an address cannot easily be traced back if someone makes even a minimal effort to hide his or her identity. Free e-mail accounts can be obtained nearly instantly using services such as Hotmail and Gmail without the need to verify one's identity. E-mail messages can be sent through *anonymous remailers* that strip all record of the sender's identity. Internet domain names can be purchased anonymously and then used to host blogs and other Web sites without revealing the identity of the author. Even if an e-mail service provider or Web site hosting company keeps records of its customers, it may be necessary to obtain a court order to divulge such records, and if the company is located in a foreign country, it may be difficult or impossible to obtain such an order.

The same features of the Internet that make it easy to remain anonymous also make it easy to impersonate another person. In particular, Web sites, e-mail messages, instant messages, and other text-based communications on the Internet do not carry with them the face, voice, or other personally identifiable features of the author that people use to recognize each other in the offline world. As a result, if one were to obtain the username and password to someone else's account on a social networking Web site, one could use this information to log in to the site as that person and then send messages under that person's name. Since the recipients would only see the text of such messages, it would be difficult for them to tell that the messages were not in fact sent by the person listed on the messages as the sender. Thus, privacy, anonymity, and identity theft are closely linked on the Internet.

The question remains whether it is necessarily unethical to use someone else's e-mail account or social networking account. If ethics is concerned with actions that cause harm, then use of another person's account is only unethical if it is harmful. Certainly there are circumstances in which impersonating someone else online can cause harm, such as when the impersonation is performed to contact the impersonated person's bank and thereby obtain financial information illicitly or when the impersonator contacts a trusted friend of the victim to obtain well-guarded secrets. In other cases, however, the impersonator might simply be playing a harmless prank for the amusement of everyone involved, including the person whose account was used. As another example, one sibling might log into her sister's account on Amazon.com to make a purchase using her sister's credit card and then pay her back in cash a few days later. Even if the actions taken in some of these cases might be considered foolish or lacking in judgment, they may not necessarily be unethical, and those that are unethical are not all unethical to the same degree.

Furthermore, one must ask whether the online community is now so well aware of how easy it is to impersonate others that acts of impersonation have begun to lose their effectiveness. If an employee receives a hate-filled e-mail message from her boss at work, she might conclude that she is most likely the victim of a hoax rather than the recipient of her boss's wrath, given how easy such hoaxes are to perpetuate. The ease of online impersonation, however, may take the sting out of any harm caused by such impersonation, at least if the intended target is sufficiently technologically sophisticated. Yet this raises the question whether the increasing sophistication of Internet users should let online imposters off the ethical hook for the consequences of their actions.

Despite such hypothetical considerations, in reality impersonating someone online can have a number of harmful consequences. For example, if one were to send hurtful or embarrassing messages in the guise of another person, such actions could have negative effects on that person's reputation, their relationships with their friends and colleagues, or even their own self-esteem. The person could feel angry, threatened, or harassed at being targeted in this manner, particularly if the identity of the impersonator remains unknown. It might be difficult for the impersonated person to be able to prove to others that he or she was not actually responsible for the messages sent. Even if such proof could be provided, some lingering ill will might remain, however irrational. For example, those who were targeted by the imposter might blame the victim of identity theft for failing to take sufficient precautions to protect his or her account from being compromised.

Furthermore, impersonating someone online could make others falsely believe that the person holds certain views or behaves in particular ways. Even small, seemingly harmless acts of impersonation, such as updating someone else's social networking profile with an embarrassing statement, could have unintended consequences. In 2007, the British online technology publication *The Register* posted an article describing how employers were beginning to use social networking Web sites to aid them in the hiring process, often examining the profiles of potential employees. However, if those profiles contained damaging statements posted by someone else (an impersonator), such statements could negatively affect these potential employees' job opportunities. The impact of such harm can be difficult to remediate because it can be difficult or impossible to delete statements from the Internet completely and permanently, since much content, once posted, is quickly backed up and copied to many locations.

Therefore, postings that originally were intended as a temporary prank may become a permanent mar on one's online persona.

Other more serious acts of impersonation, such as buying products online in another person's name, could be considered stealing, which is clearly unethical. Although making such purchases does not involve taking money from the other person in the same way as taking dollar bills from the person's wallet, the two acts are similar in the sense that both involve using someone else's money without that person's permission. One might even argue that the online act is a more serious ethical violation because it combines theft of money with identity theft and therefore could harm the victim not only by depriving them of funds but also by negatively impacting their reputation if, for example, the online transaction goes sour and causes the compromised e-commerce account to be terminated or the impersonated person's credit score to be lowered. At the same time, personal and cultural norms must be taken into account when determining whether and to what extent such actions are unethical. For example, members of a family may explicitly or implicitly give each other permission to make purchases using the e-commerce accounts of other family members. Even if granting such permission relieves members of the family of their ethical obligations to each other, it raises the question whether the family itself has caused any harm to the e-commerce merchant. For example, the merchant may have granted an account to the parents in the family based on their credit rating and the assumption that only responsible adults would make purchases from the site. If other family members then make purchases in irresponsible ways, such as by receiving a product, damaging it, and then returning it for a refund while claiming that it arrived damaged, then the interfamily agreement to share accounts has harmed the merchant and therefore arguably is unethical.

Even when sharing account information in ways that are ethical, it is important to do so cautiously. For example, although sharing an online account with someone else might be convenient and not cause any harm directly, making multiple copies of usernames, passwords, and other account information and sharing such information among multiple people can increase the likelihood that such information will be stolen by a real identity thief, who may then use such information for more malicious purposes. For this and other reasons, it is

(continues on page 16)

001101010010100111010110101010101011001010000 1

Deborah Johnson (University of Virginia Professor of Applied Ethics, Expert on Computer Ethics)

Deborah Johnson is a philosopher who specializes in professional ethics, specifically in ethical issues related to computers and information technology. She is the Anne Shirley Carter Olsson Professor of Applied Ethics and the chairwoman of the department of science, technology, and society in the School of Engineering and Applied Science of the University of Virginia.

Professor Johnson attended Monteith College, Wayne State University, and received her Ph.D. in 1976 from the University of Kansas. She spent 20 years of her academic career at the Rensselaer Polytechnic Institute, serving as the chairwoman of the department of science and technology studies, professor of philosophy and science, technology, and society, as well as an associate dean for the School of Humanities. She moved to the Georgia Institute of Technology to become a professor in the School of Public Policy as well as the director of the master's program in public policy in 1998. In 2001, Johnson arrived at the University of Virginia.

University of Virginia professor Deborah Johnson, an expert in computer ethics   *(Deborah Johnson)*

Professor Johnson became interested in the areas of information and computer ethics in the 1980s, when the field did not yet truly exist, and became one of the powerful forces that shaped it. Her 1985 book *Computer Ethics* was the first textbook in the field and remains one of the major defining works in computer ethics. Johnson defined computer ethics as a branch of ethics that examines the problems posed by new technology and applies existing moral and ethical theories in this brand-new environ-

001101010010100111010110101010101011001010000 1

ment. She disagreed with the view that held that computers generate completely new ethical problems, which was advocated by Walter Maner in the 1970s. Johnson postulated that technology transformed old ethical issues in new and sometimes unexpected ways, but believed that computer technology did not create unique and brand-new ethical problems. In later editions of *Computer Ethics,* she conceded that some specific ethical questions have been generated entirely by the newly available technology, such as software ownership and threats posed by databases to privacy, but argued that these questions were merely new versions of the previously existing questions of privacy and intellectual property. The latest (fourth) edition of *Computer Ethics* focuses on the idea of computer technology as sociotechnical systems, a "set of social practices in which hardware and software are embedded." Johnson finds the conceptual link between ethics and developing technology to be the most challenging issue in modern information technology.

Professor Johnson received several National Science Foundation grants and spent the academic 1992–93 year as a visiting professor at Princeton University working on a project on ethics and computer decision models. She received more funding from the NSF in 1994 and 1995 to conduct workshops for undergraduate faculty on teaching courses on computer and professional ethics. Between 2000 and 2003, Johnson worked on another NSF project that offered Web-based computer ethics workshops.

Professor Johnson has published more than 50 papers in multiple journals, including the prestigious *Communications of the ACM,* authored more than a half-dozen books, and received multiple awards for her contributions to the field of computer ethics. Her latest work, an edited volume of readings on history, philosophy, ethics, and politics of technology entitled *Technology and Society: Engineering Our Sociotechnical Future,* was published in November 2008. Professor Johnson coedits an international journal *Ethics and Information Technology* and has served as the editor of other respected publications in the field of computer ethics and philosophy. She also coedits a book series on women, gender, and technology for the University of Illinois Press. At the University of Virginia, Professor Johnson taught courses that focused on the interrelationship between technology and ethics, ethical theory, values, and policy. Professor

(continues)

00110101001010011101011010101010101100101000001

(continued)

Johnson received the ACM SIGCAS Making a Difference Award in 2000, the Sterling Olmstead Award from the liberal education division of the American Society for Engineering Education in 2001, and the prestigious John Barwise Prize from the American Philosophical Association in 2004. She is also active in professional organizations and served on the board of governors of the National Institute for Engineering Ethics, chaired the American Philosophical Association subcommittee on Computer Use and Philosophy, served as president of the Society for Philosophy and Technology, and as president of the International Society for Ethics and Information (INSEIT), which is the professional organization for the field of computer ethics.

00110101001010011101011010101010101100101000001

(continued from page 13)

never appropriate to pressure anyone else into sharing his or her username and password to a computer, e-mail account, Web site, or other account.

Clearly, adopting someone else's online identity is a difficult issue to navigate. The potential harms are real and extensive and the ethical dilemmas no less so. At the same time, perhaps surprisingly, online identities may be shared among multiple people in ways that are not necessarily unethical. However, given the potential for harm, anyone considering taking on someone else's identity online for a seemingly innocuous purpose would do well to stop for a long pause and extensively consider the possible outcomes before moving forward.

PRIVACY IN THE WORKPLACE

More than 77 million people use a computer at work in the United States, and nearly all of these have access to the Internet through their work computers. Unless employers take active steps to limit the ability of employees to make personal use of the Internet, employees may use their Internet connection at work to send and receive personal e-mail, conduct personal online banking, communicate with friends using social networking sites, and engage in holiday shopping.

This does not necessarily imply that all personal use of computers by employees is wrong. It may be perfectly permissible to send and receive personal e-mail using a company computer during a lunch break or to conduct online shopping from home using a mobile phone provided by the employer, if the employer did not instruct the employee that such activities are prohibited.

Employers, however, have legitimate reasons to prohibit employees from making certain kinds of uses of computers during work hours and when using the employer's computer equipment off-site. First and foremost, employees are hired and paid to perform certain tasks for their employers. Employees who spend time at work engaging in personal computer and Internet use are not doing their jobs. Therefore, there is some validity to the complaint by employers that personal Internet use by employees is like stealing from the employer, because such employees are being paid to engage in personal tasks rather than performing the responsibilities that they are paid to perform. Second, to the extent that time spent surfing the Web and performing other non-work-related tasks reduces employees' productivity, excessive Internet use by employees can reduce the employer's profits. This can harm not only the owners of the company but also its shareholders and other employees. Finally, employees who work in safety-critical positions, such as bus drivers, air traffic controllers, or electric power plant managers, need to remain sharply focused throughout the workday. Engaging in Web browsing, text messaging, and personal phone calling can distract such employees from their primary task and lead to injuries or death.

Despite such risks, it is not practical for employers to prevent employees from engaging in all computer and Internet use. Employers want and need to provide their employees with access to computers and the Internet to help them perform their jobs. Most office workers today need to have access to e-mail and the Web to communicate with colleagues and customers, perform research, plan business trips, and perform other business-related tasks that would be significantly more time-consuming and costly to perform without the Internet. A 911 operator may be able to help provide emergency services more quickly and effectively by having access to a Web browser for helping ambulance drivers find alternate routes to a crime victim in the face of a traffic jam.

The problem for employers, therefore, is that although there are significant benefits to providing employees with Internet access, such access also enables employees to engage in a wide variety of personal activities which, before the advent of the Internet, would have been difficult or impossible for employees to perform while on the employer's premises during work hours. Although some technological tools exist that employers can use to limit the kinds of Internet-related activities employees can engage in while at work, such tools tend to be very blunt. For example, employers can install Web site–filtering software on the employer's computers to block employees from visiting certain Web sites (such as YouTube, Facebook, and video game sites), but such tools can prevent employees from engaging in legitimate work-related activity. For example, a marketing executive may find it useful to communicate with prospective customers on Facebook.

Therefore, an increasing number of employers have decided that it is more effective to monitor their employees' computer and Internet use than to block it. Employers can engage in such monitoring by installing a variety of different kinds of *spyware* software on their computer systems to track employees' computer usage and to report on such usage to the employer. For example, *key loggers* record the keys pressed by employees while typing e-mail messages, text messages, and word processing documents. *Web-monitoring software* tracks the Web sites visited by employees. Such software can be configured not only to create a complete log of all of the employees' activities, but also to send an alert to the employer upon detecting specific activity by an employee, such as the use of racist language in an e-mail message or the visiting of a pornography Web site. Approximately 78 percent of employers engage in this practice at some level, with 36 percent admitting to storing and perusing the computer files of employees.

Such monitoring of employees by employers typically has been held to be lawful, at least if the employer previously disclosed to employees that the employer uses monitoring software or reserves the right to do so. Typically, employers are permitted by law to monitor the activities of their employees, except in a narrow range of circumstances, such as while employees are in the bathroom.

Whether such monitoring is ethical is a separate question. One could review all of the reasons provided above for concluding that personal Internet use by employees is legitimate or illegitimate and conclude that monitoring employees either is unethical or ethical for the same reasons. However, such monitoring remains particularly controversial, perhaps because it is not clear whether the mere fact that an employee is engaged in prohibited behavior—such as online shopping during work hours—justifies monitoring all activities of the employee throughout the entire workday.

This disconnect, and resulting difficulty in determining whether monitoring of employees is ethical, may arise in part from the fact that until recently it was relatively difficult and expensive for employers to monitor employees. Monitoring required the installation of large, expensive, and clunky security cameras, which recorded information onto videotapes that could only store a relatively small amount of information. Furthermore, reviewing such videotapes was very time-consuming, and as a result review was not performed except in response to suspicion of employee theft or some other problem necessitating review. As a result, very few employers attempted to monitor their employees. Therefore, the question of whether such monitoring was ethical did not frequently arise as a practical matter.

Furthermore, even when monitoring was performed, it was relatively apparent to employees that they were being monitored. They could see the video cameras pointed at them, and they could easily know when they were in a room lacking video cameras. In contrast, employer spyware usually operates without giving the employee any indication that it is tracking the employee's activity. Even though the employer may have formally notified the employee that spyware was in use or might be used, such notification seems different from the unavoidable presence of a large video camera with a red light in the corner of a room. As a result, modern monitoring techniques raise concerns about whether employees truly are aware that they are being monitored and whether, as a result, they might engage in personal activities (such as communicating with their doctors) and thereby expose private information to their employers unintentionally.

The situation is further complicated by the fact that employers, at least in some situations, may either be required to monitor their employees or at least face criticism or even legal action for failing to monitor their employees. For example, a company that operates in a highly regulated industry, such as securities trading, may be required by law to provide certain information to its customers in all communications. Therefore, the employer may have good reason to monitor all telephone calls and e-mail messages between employees and customers and to use software to analyze such communications to ensure that they satisfy all applicable legal requirements. As another example, an employer who detects harassing e-mail messages sent by one employee to another may reduce its legal liability if it takes swift and effective action to punish the harasser. Yet it is difficult, if not impossible, for employers to monitor and analyze employee communications for such legitimate purposes without also monitoring and analyzing messages that contain private information.

As the examples above illustrate, it is difficult to draw clear conclusions about the propriety of monitoring employee computer use. In response to this difficulty, many employers have developed *employer privacy policies* that include descriptions of content that is forbidden for employees to access, such as pornographic content, game sites, entertainment, shopping, and personal e-mail. Typically, employees are given a copy of the policy at the start of their employment and required to sign a statement confirming that they have read the policy, understand it, and will comply with it. Although it is not possible for such policies to eliminate all ethical gray areas, they at least can provide some bright lines that employees can follow so that they do not need to rely on their own personal judgments about the answers to tricky ethical questions.

The rapid rise in use of social networking sites only complicates the situation. In recent years, employees have begun displaying more and more personal information about themselves online, such as on personal Web pages, blogs, and online social networks, such as LinkedIn and Facebook. As a result, a whole new set of ethical questions has emerged. For example, there is much debate over whether it is ethical for employees to provide information about their employers or to express criticism of their employers on social networking sites if they provide such information during off-work hours. The flip side of this question is whether employers are justified in disciplining or even firing employees who post such information. Some argue that entries on social networking pages are like office chat around the water cooler, while others argue that it is more similar to publishing an editorial in a national newspaper. This is yet another example where the inability to draw clear analogies between current electronic media and older paper-based and personal communication leads to difficulty in drawing ethical conclusions about modern communications.

In order to address this issue, many employers are now requiring employees to sign specific agreements about the use of online social networks, detailing what such employees may and may not share on their profiles, regardless of where and when they post the information. For example, all Sears and Kmart employees are now required to sign agreements that prevent them from posting negative comments about the company or sharing *confidential information.* Despite many employees' cries of First Amendment violations, maintain that these constitutional provisions only apply to the public sector, not to private employers. Still, the ethical debate continues.

IS IT EVER UNETHICAL TO KEEP INFORMATION PRIVATE?

The right to privacy might seem to imply that keeping information private is not only a legal right but also inherently an ethical act or at least not an unethical act. For example, if someone chooses not to reveal the contents of his or her personal diary to others, we would not consider such secrecy to be unethical. In fact, if someone else distributed the diary to the public without the owner's permission, such an act would be highly unethical. Similarly, if an employee of a company refuses to disclose the company's customer list or other trade secrets, we would commend such an act as not only lawful but ethical.

Yet the situation is not so simple, because privacy and ethics are not necessarily consistent with each other in all circumstances. For example, in democracies and other open societies, the government generally has an obligation to make its decisions and the facts and reasoning underlying such decisions available to the public. If there is a law prohibiting stealing, the existence of such a law should be known to the public, so that people cannot be prosecuted and convicted for violating the law without having an opportunity to know in advance that their actions were unlawful. Similarly, when Congress or another legislature debates a potential new law, such debates should be open to the public. Court proceedings, except in exceptional circumstances, should also be open to the public, and judges should be required to publicly state both their decisions and the reasons for their decisions. Such openness helps members of the public participate in their own government and protects against government corruption. It is more difficult for a judge to make a decision based on a bribe, rather than on the requirements of the law, if the judge must spell out the reasons for his or her decision in a written document that is available for the public to inspect.

In addition to the general requirement that government actions be taken publicly, various special laws have been passed in the United States to promote further openness. For example, the federal *Freedom of Information Act (FOIA)* entitles members of the public to request and obtain information from federal agencies, such as reports generated by such agencies for use in drafting legislation and records of government activities, such as surveys, searches, and censuses. The Freedom of Information Act is a kind of *sunshine law,* other examples of which entitle members of the public to attend government meetings and obtain records of public proceedings.

When a member of the public submits a request for information to the government, sunshine laws typically require the government to provide the requested information to the requester, unless the law provides a valid reason not to provide the information, in which case the government official handling the request is required to provide that reason to the requester when refusing to provide the information. The government's refusal to provide information that is required by law is an unlawful act. A more difficult question is whether it is also unethical. One could argue that such a refusal is unethical because, by withholding information from a member of the public, the government is impeding the public's ability to take part in the democratic process.

The law itself, however, recognizes many exceptions to sunshine laws. For example, under the Freedom of Information Act, the government is not required to provide information that is protected by the trade secret rights of a private party. For example, the government is not required to turn over the secret formula to a chemical used to deice the wings of military aircraft if the formula is the trade secret of a private corporation. Whether maintaining the secrecy of such information is ethical is a more difficult question, because it involves balancing the rights of the corporation against the rights of the individual. Although one could argue that the rights of the individual citizen should always trump the rights of a corporation, if the government were to routinely turn over trade secrets to the public, companies would likely stop sharing such trade secrets with the government, thereby depriving the public of the benefit of such trade secrets.

Similar considerations apply to information in the possession of the government that contains sensitive facts about individuals, such as their Social Security numbers, medical history, and criminal records. Whether it is ethical to reveal such information can be particularly difficult to determine if the request for such information is made for the purpose of protecting public safety or uncovering government incompetence or corruption. For example, a citizen watchdog group might request the medical records of members of the National Guard to determine whether work they have performed at the sites of natural disasters has harmed their health, thereby entitling them to government health benefits that they have been denied.

As another example, lawyers have both a legal and ethical obligation to maintain their clients' confidentiality. The purpose of such lawyer-client confidentiality—and the related concept of attorney-client privilege, which specifically protects attorney-client communications from being disclosed in court proceedings—is to ensure that a client is comfortable being completely open so that the lawyer can provide advice that is based on the full set of relevant facts. Clients may seek out legal advice in connection with criminal or otherwise unlawful acts. As a general rule, the lawyer is required to keep secret even the client's admission that he or she has engaged in criminal acts, such as theft, robbery, or even murder. If the client were to make such an admission to her lawyer and the lawyer were to reveal the admission to a third party—even to a judge—without the client's fully informed consent, the lawyer would be disciplined and possibly even prohibited from practicing law in the future. The bond of confidentiality between lawyer and client surpasses even that of parent and child or husband and wife in the eyes of the law.

Yet even lawyer-client confidentiality has exceptions that were created to allow the lawyer to disclose confidential client information in those rare circumstances in which keeping the client's secrets would clearly be unethical. The most notable exception requires the attorney to reveal information obtained from the client if the attorney reasonably believes that revealing such information is necessary to prevent the client from committing a criminal act that the lawyer reasonably believes is likely to result in death or substantial bodily harm to another person. For example, if the client tells the lawyer that he plans to murder someone later that day, the lawyer is required to inform the police of this plan.

Note, however, just how narrow this exception is—the lawyer is not required to reveal *past* criminal activity by the client, such as a past theft or murder, no matter how heinous. Furthermore, the lawyer is not required to disclose future crimes planned by the client if the lawyer does not reasonably believe that such crimes are likely to result in death or substantial bodily injury. Under this rule, for example, the lawyer would not be required to—and would in fact be prohibited from—revealing that the client plans to steal a car.

001101010010100111010110101010101011001010000 1

Enron, WorldCom, and Arthur Andersen

Enron and Worldcom are now practically synonymous with scandal. However, this was not always the case. Before 2001, Enron and Worldcom were among the most profitable companies in the world. Enron was a major energy corporation, and Worldcom operated in the field of telecommunications. Both companies had heavily traded stock, with Enron's stock reaching $90 per share in 2000. Enron, in particular, was widely praised and admired for its innovative technology and business model. It was even cited as a model for other utility companies to follow in the future.

In October 2001, however, the discovery of a number of under-the-table deals, accounting irregularities, and other questionable activities tarnished Enron's reputation. It came to light that executives had intentionally covered up an enormous quantity of debt, defrauding investors and inflating the value of their company. Similarly, in 2002, a team of auditors uncovered fraudulent practices at Worldcom, discovering that the company had been masking its declining value through faulty accounting and underreported expenses. Both corporations eventually filed for bankruptcy amid a torrent of negative press, legal allegations, and public dismay.

This, however, was not the whole story. As the Enron scandal unfolded, the press as well as the SEC launched an investigation to determine the extent to which accounting firm and consulting company Arthur Andersen was involved in the fraudulent practices. Under normal circumstances, it would have been Andersen's job to certify that the company's accounting methods were sound and their reports accurate and honest. However, seeing an opportunity to increase their fee, the firm remained silent. When it became clear that the SEC would be investigating their role, officials at Andersen reportedly went on a document-destruction

001101010010100111010110101010101011001010000 1

Although the public generally recognizes and agrees with the need for lawyers to maintain their clients' confidentiality, the unusual nature of this obligation often causes controversy. Lawyers who represent criminal clients often face public criticism when they staunchly defend their clients' confidentiality, especially if their clients continue to commit additional crimes. The argument is often made that such lawyers should reveal what they know about their clients'

1001110100101010100110010111011010100101001

rampage, shredding an enormous quantity of paper and deleting a large number of e-mail messages related to the Enron account. In June 2002, Andersen was convicted of obstruction of justice, although this ruling was later overturned by the Supreme Court due to irregularities in jury instructions. When the Worldcom scandal erupted, Andersen became implicated as well. Although the firm's officials formally denied guilt, Worldcom investors, as well as members of the press and the public, vilified the company.

Due to the Supreme Court's ruling, Andersen was legally allowed to resume business. However, the firm's activities have dwindled significantly as a result of its connection to scandal. While once thought of as an authority on auditing, accounting, and consulting practices, the company is now primarily known for its proximity to scandal. The company's story acts a solemn reminder to other firms, suggesting the need for clear document-retention policies. By failing to preserve documents, companies can risk legal liability if those documents in any way could have aided the discovery of evidence in trial. Furthermore, accounting companies or those who perform similar services particularly rely on an impeccable reputation for honesty and integrity. Their entire business is based on faith in their decision-making processes. Andersen's story is a cautionary tale about what can happen to an accounting and auditing firm when it steps too far over the line. It is also a story about technology, because now that we live in the day of electronic forensics, it can be nearly impossible to destroy electronic documents in a way that cannot later be uncovered by trained and diligent experts. Therefore, even those who lack the ethical judgment to retain harmful documents would be wise to avoid the temptation to destroy such documents, simply because doing so is extremely unlikely to successfully hide evidence of misconduct and is likely to lead to charges not only of misconduct but also of engaging in a cover-up of that misconduct.

1001110100101010100110010111011010100101001

past actions and future plans, at least to a judge or to law enforcement authorities, to protect public safety. As these and other examples illustrate, the general rule that it is ethical to keep private information private does not necessarily apply in all circumstances. Especially when public safety is at stake, it can be particularly difficult to determine whether the most ethical course of action is to reveal information or keep it secret.

DESTROYING INFORMATION

Prior to the growth of computer technology, it was unimaginable that our society would have the record-keeping capabilities available now. After all, information stored in human memories tends to fade and distort over time, just as information stored on paper is susceptible to loss and damage by the elements. Information stored on computers, however, tends to persist for a very long time, particularly if it is backed up, transmitted over the Internet, and stored in multiple places along the way. While a note written from John to Jane on paper might only be stored in Jane's office, an e-mail message would automatically remain stored on John's computer, Jane's computer, and the e-mail servers of both their Internet service providers. Computers and the Internet, therefore, raise difficult questions about when we are ethically required or permitted to destroy or retain information.

Most people agree that an individual has the right to decide when to destroy and when to retain his or her own personal information, such as photographs he or she has taken. The question becomes more difficult, however, when the information is related to a business, a branch of the government, or some issue of concern to the public. For example, it is not clear whether an individual is morally obligated to retain information that could possibly be of use for the public good in the future or whether that person could be deemed at fault for accidentally destroying such information.

In addition, most people agree that it is ethical to destroy information in one's possession that contains private data about others once that information is no longer in use. For example, a business may need to obtain the credit card number of a customer in order to process a purchase from that customer. However, once the transaction is complete and the time has expired for the customer to return the purchased product, it is not only prudent but ethical for the business to delete the customer's credit card information so that it does not remain susceptible to capture by identity thieves.

Similarly, most people agree that it would be unethical to destroy information that could be used for someone else's benefit in the future. For example, although hospitals obtain highly private information about their patients, it would be considered unethical for hospitals to delete such information, even many years after it was first obtained, because information about a patient's medical history may be necessary for providing health care to the patient in the future. The amount of time that a particular piece of information must be retained, however, depends on the length of the information's useful life.

Given all of these factors, deciding what to retain and what to destroy can often be difficult. For companies, many legal organizations such as the American Bar Association recommend creating a very specific *document retention policy* to protect against any lawsuits involving the destruction or retention of information. Such policies generally include specific protocols for filtering e-mail communication and documents (for example, retaining any e-mail messages containing keywords that suggest they contain sensitive information). While clearly not all information can (or should) be saved, companies that employ conservative information-destruction policies generally report that they are happy to have saved so much material. When weighing the many ethical dilemmas, most sources agree: When in doubt, keep it.

CONCLUSIONS

Although the difficult choices faced by private individuals, employers, corporate executives, government officials, and attorneys when determining whether to reveal otherwise confidential information to the public existed long before computers and the Internet, the widespread adoption of such technologies exacerbate the ethical problems. In the Internet age, once information is revealed to one person, it is likely to be made available instantly to the world. As Warren and Brandeis foresaw, "What is whispered in the closet shall be proclaimed from the house-tops." The government official who is deciding whether to distribute the blueprints for a water treatment plant to an environmental organization must now take into account whether doing so will make the same blueprints available over the Internet to terrorist organizations who wish to attack the plant, and the lawyer who is considering whether to disclose the possible future criminal activity of her client must take into account whether doing so will prevent that client from ever obtaining a fair jury trial once the revealed information becomes available to the general public after being distributed over the Web. Whether or not "privacy is dead," as Scott McNealy proclaimed, the Internet certainly does make the conditions of privacy's continued existence more ethically complex than ever before.

2

SECURITY: CHALLENGES IN THE INFORMATION SOCIETY

Computer viruses can spread automatically in a variety of ways, such as by attaching themselves to e-mail messages. Although it may seem clear that it is not ethical to intentionally spread a harmful virus, the more difficult question is whether computer users have an ethical obligation to protect their computers against viruses and other attacks, such as by installing the latest antivirus software on their computers. Although this may at first seem to be only a question of prudence, not ethics, someone who fails to install antivirus software unwittingly exposes his or her computer to being hijacked by viruses, which can then spread to other computers. Therefore, it is at least arguable that computer users have an ethical obligation to secure their own computers to protect the computers of others.

Some even argue that there are situations in which it is ethically permissible to unleash a virus onto the Internet. For example, some computer security experts claim that by publishing information about security weaknesses in Microsoft Windows and by releasing viruses that expose such weaknesses they push Microsoft to patch the operating system so that it is protected against such viruses, thereby improving the operating system's security. The result is a more secure version of Microsoft Windows for everyone, and therefore the net effect of having released the virus may be positive. Yet publishing information about security flaws and releasing viruses that exploit those flaws also gives ammunition to identity thieves to spread viruses to steal credit card information and other sensitive data. This chapter will explore the complex interconnections between computer security and ethics, with reference to real-world examples of incidents that have sparked controversy.

Computer security is threefold. It may refer to:

(1) the integrity and security of the data that resides on an individual computer;
(2) the physical security of the computer itself; or
(3) the security of the network to which the computer is connected.

Although these three aspects of computer security may be analyzed distinctly, they also interrelate. The security of the data on the individual computer depends on the user's perception of the security of the physical computer and the security of the network; a user is less likely to be willing to provide accurate information if he does not believe that the information can be adequately protected from misuse or theft. In that respect, security intersects with privacy.

The following sections explore these three aspects of computer security and their ethical implications.

SECURITY OF THE INDIVIDUAL COMPUTER

As mentioned above, one aspect of computer security is the physical security of the individual computer. The techniques for maintaining security have not changed much since the early days of computers. The physical security of computers today is protected by physically locking computers to walls, floors, desks, and other immovable objects so that they become difficult to move or steal. Locks may also be placed on the housing of the computer so that no one without a key can open the housing and inspect or remove equipment, such as hard disk drives containing sensitive data.

One relatively recent development in physical computer security is the use of global positioning system (GPS) technology within computers that can detect the geographical location of a stolen computer and report it back to the lawful owner or a security firm to assist in tracking down the computer and prosecuting the thief. To protect the computer itself, some brands such as the Panasonic Toughbook are physically designed to be resistant to damage from wind, rain, falls, and other harsh conditions and are particularly well-suited for use by field scientists, workers in the construction industry, and those who travel in varying environments.

Most efforts at securing the computer, however, relate not to the physical security of the computer but to maintaining the integrity and security of the data stored on the computer. *Data integrity* refers to the extent to which the data remains unchanged over time, so that its contents may be relied on to be accurate. Analog cassette tapes do not have high integrity, because they tend to degrade over time. As a result, playing back an old cassette tape tends to yield music that sounds distorted. Similarly, computer hard disk drives need to be replaced periodically, because the data they contain remains intact only for so long. After some amount of time, which can vary widely from drive to drive, data may become spontaneously and unpredictably corrupted, thereby making it impossible to rely on. This can have significantly harmful consequences if financial, medical, or other critical records are stored. One common way to protect data integrity is to use multiple hard disk drives that are configured always to contain exact copies of the same data. Then a computer can continuously compare the data on both hard drives and detect if the two ever differ. The drive containing the error can then be identified, such as by comparing the contents of both hard drives to a recent backup. The faulty drive can then be replaced. One such technology is known as Redundant Array of Independent Disks (RAID), now available even on relatively low-end home computers.

The security of data stored on the individual computer *(data security)* refers to the extent to which the data are protected against access by parties who are unauthorized. One common and simple example of protection of data security is the use of usernames and passwords that must be entered into a computer before a user is provided with access to data on the computer. The success of such a scheme relies on a variety of factors, such as the use of strong passwords (i.e., passwords that are difficult to guess), protection against theft of passwords, and the difficulty of cracking the software that denies access to those who do not provide a legitimate username and password.

Many users defeat the security function of passwords by using their first name, pet's name, or telephone number as a password. Such passwords are not secure because anyone who knows the computer's owner can easily guess these kind of passwords in just a few tries, thereby enabling them to obtain unauthorized access to the owner's computer. Security experts recommend avoiding such passwords and even recommend not using any word in the dictionary as a password because a technically savvy person intent on guessing such a password can use software to quickly try all of the words in the dictionary as passwords in an attempt to break into a computer. Instead, a secure password consists of a random string of characters, including uppercase and lowercase letters, numbers, and special characters (such as !, @, #, $, and %). It should also be at least six, and preferably at least 10, characters long. If a random string of characters is too difficult to remember, the next best technique is to choose an obscure word that is easy for the user to remember but difficult for others to guess, spell it backwards, make at least one of its characters uppercase and at least one other lowercase, and add at least two nonalphanumeric characters, such as punctuation marks. Such passwords can be easy to remember with a little practice but extremely difficult to guess, even by software.

Another common way to protect the security of data is to encrypt (scramble) it so that even if someone else obtains access to the data, that person is unable to make sense of it without also obtaining access to the corresponding decryption key. Some operating systems include built-in encryption features, such as Mac OS X's FileVault and Windows 7's BitLocker. In addition, particularly safety-conscious users can employ third-party software, such as GhostSurf, eCipher, McAfee Anti-Theft File Protection, and Voltage Security Network. These packages range in price from a few dollars to upward of $80. Encryption software can be used to encrypt data stored on the computer's hard disk drive, e-mail sent and received by the computer, and even Web sites visited using the computer.

Yet another way to protect the security of data on a computer is to install antivirus software and to make sure that the antivirus software is kept up to date to protect against the latest viruses (which rapidly copy themselves, infecting networks of computers), worms (which locate backdoor *glitches* in programs), Trojan horses (which appear like harmless programs but actually provide hackers with access to computers), key loggers, and other *malware* and spyware programs. Antivirus software is an important component of an overall system for protecting data security because malware often is designed to destroy data stored on a computer or to copy such data and transmit it over the Internet to a third party for nefarious purposes.

Despite the fact that these security-enhancing techniques exist and undoubtedly are advisable, this does not answer the question whether a person is ethically required to take them. At first glance, it may seem that if someone fails to keep his or her data secure, he or she may run the risk of identity theft, an effect harmful only to that person. In reality, however, failure to secure a computer's data can harm other people in a variety of ways.

For example, even a computer that is owned and used only by a single individual often contains personal information about many other people, such as contact information and documents received in e-mail messages. Failure to keep the computer secure can put all of this data at risk, therefore harming people other than the computer's direct user by subjecting them to identity theft and other breaches of privacy. For example, the famous ILOVEYOU virus of 2000 used e-mail address books to infect entire social networks. From this perspective, it appears that the computer's user may have an ethical obligation to many other people to keep a computer secure.

In addition, many people often share a single computer, whether at home or in a workplace. If one person fails to keep antivirus software or other security mechanisms up to date, the private information of other members of the family could be compromised. Similarly, if one member of the family engages in unsafe behavior on the computer, such as by visiting Web sites that contain viruses or spyware, the computer can become infected and then perform malicious actions such as copying private data. As a result, when multiple people share one computer, each user may have an ethical responsibility to use the computer in ways that do not cause the security of data on the computer to be compromised.

The answer to this question is not straightforward, however, because there is a gap between the technical sophistication of those who create malware and the technical sophistication of the average computer user. It may be unreasonable to impose an ethical obligation on the average computer user to protect their personal computer against all possible security threats at all times, particularly given the rate at which new kinds of threats become available. Perhaps the most that can be asked of computer users is to install anti-malware software on their computers and to configure it to update itself automatically and frequently. At that point, the burden shifts to the vendors of anti-malware software to ensure that they use their technical skills to protect the public against dangerous security threats.

`1001110100101010100110010111011010100101001`

Internet Viruses and Information Phishing Schemes

Most computer users today have at least heard of the dangers of computer viruses, but many may not understand the technical details underlying how viruses work and the methods by which they are spread. Essentially, a computer virus is a program that is capable of replicating (copying) itself, transmitting itself from one computer to another, and installing itself on the computers to which it is transmitted. One way in which viruses are transmitted is by including them as *e-mail attachments*. Such attachments typically are disguised as legitimate files, such as word processing documents or videos, which the recipient is enticed to open. Once opened, the virus installs itself on the recipient's computer, typically without providing any indication to the user that this is happening. To enable itself to replicate, the virus may install a program on the computer that causes all future outgoing e-mail messages sent by that computer to contain the virus as an attachment. In this way, the virus spreads from computer to computer, not only without the knowledge of those who receive the virus, but also without the knowledge of those who unwittingly retransmit the virus to others. Some viruses may even automatically retransmit themselves, such as by generating e-mail messages to everyone in the end user's address book, but without providing any indication that such e-mail messages are being sent. Examples of famous viruses include the Melissa virus of 1999, the ILOVEYOU virus of 2000, the Code Red and Nimda viruses of 2001, and the Sasser virus of 2004.

The *payload* of the virus is the portion of the virus that performs the function for which the virus was designed. Such functions can vary from the annoying, such as displaying a funny or offensive message on the screen that the user cannot remove without deleting the virus, to the harmful, such as copying personal information from the user's computer (such as financial data and Social Security numbers) and transmitting this information back to the virus's creator, destroying data on the computer, or even corrupting the operating system so that the computer ceases to function. Some in the computer hacking community consider the spread of viruses of the annoying variety to be harmless fun and a sign of one's

(continues)

`1001110100101010100110010111011010100101001`

programming skill. Others consider disseminating any kind of virus, no matter its function, to be unethical because the mere act of spreading a virus takes control of someone else's computer without that person's permission and in some cases without that person's knowledge.

Phishing schemes, on the other hand, trick users into divulging sensitive information by misleading them into providing this information to an identity thief or other con artist, under the belief that they are providing the information to a trusted party. For example, someone might perpetrate a phishing scam by sending e-mail messages to customers of a bank, where the e-mail messages appear to originate from the bank, warning the customers that they must update their usernames and passwords to protect the security of their accounts. Recipients of such an e-mail message, believing it to be from the bank, might click on a link in the e-mail message that directs them to a site that looks identical to the bank's homepage, but which is in fact a Web site operated by the phishing scheme's perpetrator. The address of the Web site may even be similar to, but slightly different from, that of the bank, such as www.bankofamerica.biz instead of www. bankofamerica.com, thereby leading inattentive readers to mistake one for the other. Sometimes the actual address of the legitimate Web site appears within the address of the fake Web site, as in the case of www.zyx.com/www.bankofamerica. com.html. Unsophisticated users might think that the presence of "www.bank ofamerica.com" within the address proves the legitimacy of the address, when in fact the page they are visiting is a page within the imposter's Web site.

Should the user then enter his or her username and password or other sensitive information such as bank account number into the Web page, such information would then be sent straight to the creators of the phishing scheme. The phishing Web site might even display a phony confirmation message, further lulling the user into a false sense of security. The phishing operator can then use the user's information to log into the user's real bank account to steal money or commit other types of fraud and identity theft.

Other recent phishing attacks include e-mail messages disguised as tax-related communications from the U.S. Internal Revenue Service (IRS) and schemes that steal log-in information for social networking sites. One of the most widespread phishing schemes occurred in 2006, targeting users with Myspace profile pages. The scam began when users received e-mail messages directing them to a Myspace look-alike Web site and prompting them to enter log-in information. The data were then used to access additional personal data and to target users' social networks.

Few would dispute that phishing schemes are both unethical and unlawful. Less immediately obvious is that misleading someone to reveal their log-in information, even for innocent purposes such as a prank, can also be unethical. Obtaining someone else's log-in information creates an additional copy of this information that, if not properly secured, can then be stolen by a real identity thief for nefarious purposes. Therefore, personal log-in information should be treated with the same care and respect as documents stored in a safe deposit box in the pre-digital world.

Phishing schemes often involve sending an e-mail message that appears to originate from a legitimate and trusted source, such as a bank, university, or retail merchant, but which in fact is an attempt to lure the recipient into providing private information, such as a bank account number or Social Security number, that the phishing scammer can then use to break into the recipient's bank account or otherwise defraud the recipient. This photo shows a phishing e-mail message that appears to originate from PayPal. One piece of evidence that the e-mail message is illegitimate is the awkward wording of the subject line: "Notice of Account Review Necessity." Such warning signs can be difficult to detect and are easily overlooked.   *(Roberto Herrett/Alamy)*

SECURITY OF THE COMPUTER NETWORK

A *computer network* is any collection of computers connected to one another, whether by direct cabling or over a more sophisticated network such as a *local area network (LAN)* or the Internet. A computer network, therefore, includes not only the computers within the network but also a variety of computer hardware and software for physically connecting the computers and for enabling communications among computers in the network efficiently and effectively.

Network security is concerned with protecting an entire network of computers, whether it is a business network, a home network, or the Internet as a whole. Attacks on a computer network typically are directed at bypassing the routers, switches, and other networking hardware that is intended to protect the data stored on computers within the network. For example, such attacks may aim to disrupt the flow of information in the network by using viruses or worms that infiltrate one or more machines connected to the network and replicate themselves onto other systems within it.

In the early days of personal computers in the 1970s and 1980s, most computers were not connected to the Internet or any other network. Instead, each home computer was used to run software in isolation from other computers. As a result, the opportunities for breaches of privacy and security were much more limited than they are today. Even if someone successfully infected a computer with a virus, it was relatively unlikely that the infection would spread to other computers, because in the absence of a network connection, the only way for the virus to spread was by being passed manually from computer to computer on tapes, diskettes, or other physical storage media. Even if a virus did start to spread to multiple computers within an office in this way, the extent of the damage was limited because the virus had almost no opportunity to spread to computers located elsewhere.

In addition, people did not store as much personal information on their computers as they do today. It was common for people to use computers primarily as word processors to create and edit documents, not to store personal, sensitive information. Therefore, if the computer was infected by a virus during this period, the damage was much less significant. The most that a virus could do was damage or copy documents, not steal credit card information or disseminate private photographs over the Internet, because such information was not stored on the user's computer.

Finally, even when people did connect their computers to a network, they often did so using telephone dial-up connections, which were very slow and not continuously connected to the Internet. Instead, someone might log in to a dial-up network for 30 minutes to send and receive e-mail and then terminate the connection. As a result, the computer was exposed to network threats for a shorter period of time, reducing the likelihood of virus infection and other security breaches. Even if a computer was infected with a virus, the slow speed of the network connection limited how much data could be transmitted by the virus.

Today, of course, the landscape is quite different. According to the Pew Internet & American Life Project, 74 percent of adults in the United States reported using the Internet in December 2008, suggesting that most computers are no longer used strictly for word processing. In fact, of all Internet users, 75 percent have searched for medical information online, 71 percent have bought a product, 68 percent have made a travel reservation, and 55 percent have used online banking services. Clearly, today's computers are used to process a variety of highly sensitive information, making them all the more vulnerable to virus attacks.

In addition, much Internet traffic today is conducted using high-speed, always on network connections that constantly transmit data. This fact significantly increases the chances of network security breaches, as hackers are constantly provided with access and a high-quality data stream. This reality affects computer users in both home and business settings.

Today, viruses can spread quickly and easily across networks. Once even a small number of people become infected, the numbers increase exponentially. In addition, a whole host of new threats have emerged, including spyware, malware, worms, and Trojan horses, which disguise themselves as legitimate programs, prompting users to download and install these malicious applications to their computers. Once this occurs on a networked computer, the entire network can quickly become infected.

As such, both business network administrators and home computer users have begun increasing their network security measures. The figure on page 38 shows a diagram of a typical network security setup that uses several mechanisms as protections against network attacks, such as:

- application security, such as the requirement that a recognized username and password be provided at a computer before documents are provided to that computer;

⊕ mirrored databases, which contain exact copies of each other, so that if any one of the mirrored databases is corrupted (such as by a virus), the original data can be restored from one of the copies; and

⊕ a firewall, which blocks incoming network communication that comes from unknown or otherwise suspicious sources.

Using a variety of defenses increases the likelihood that any kind of attack against the network will either be repelled before it can succeed or at least be

(continues on page 40)

Network Security

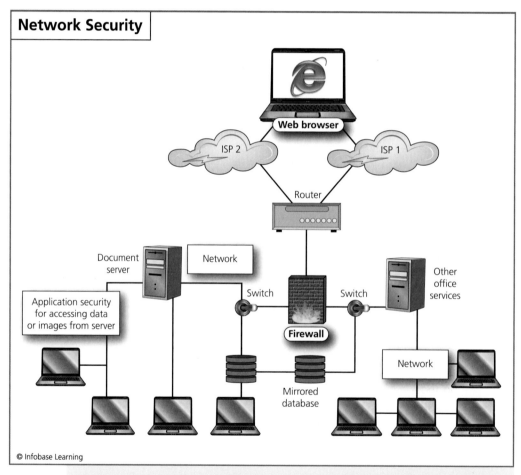

© Infobase Learning

Network security involves protecting a communications network against attacks that are intended to take harmful action against computers within the network, such as installing viruses and copying sensitive data. Because of the significant harm that successful attacks can cause, maintaining network security is no longer solely a technical or business concern; it is also an ethical concern.

`100111010010101010011001011101101010010101001`

Bruce Schneier (Computer Security Expert)

Born on January 15, 1963, in New York City, Bruce Schneier received a bachelor's degree in physics from the University of Rochester, followed by a master's degree in computer science from American University in Washington, D.C. He worked for the Department of Defense in security cryptography and deployment, followed by a stint at a start-up in Chicago, and Bell Labs before starting his own firm, Counterpane Consulting, in 1991. Counterpane Consulting became Counterpane Internet Security in 1999,

Bruce Schneier, computer security expert   *(AP Images)*

specializing in security management for network protection. In October 2006, Counterpane was acquired by BT, and is now BT Managed Security Solutions Group. Schneier is the chief technology officer at BT and resides in Minneapolis, Minnesota, with his wife.

Schneier is one of the world's top security experts and inventor of the Blowfish, MacGuffin, and Twofish ciphers (encryption/decryption algorithms), as well as the Yarrow and Fortuna cryptographically secure pseudorandom number generators. He is widely regarded as a security authority and has testified before the U.S. Congress on security matters. He has written seven books on security and cryptography. His first book, *Applied Cryptography,* is considered a definitive work in the field of cryptography; his more recent book, *Beyond Fear: Thinking Sensibly about Security in an Uncertain World,* provides a realistic guide to managing security in today's increasingly fearful world. Schneier also publishes a monthly Internet newsletter on security issues called "Crypto-Gram," and maintains a blog. He frequently speaks in public and is quoted in the media about computer and security issues.

Schneier believes that a security system must not be evaluated on the basis of how it works but by anticipating how it may fail. As such, he considers many commonly used security measures, especially the more recently introduced security

(continues)

`100111010010101010011001011101101010010101001`

0011010100101001110101101010101011001010000

(continued)

measures, unnecessary and often detrimental to achieving real security. At the same time, Schneier believes that complete security is impossible and that, as a result, a realistic approach must balance the benefits of using technology and the harms of a potential security breach of that technology. Additionally, as computers improve and become faster, Schneier predicts that the amount of computer crime will increase. Therefore, in order to remain efficient, he believes that security must be designed with the system instead of being added on to an existing system. As networks become more interconnected in the future, they will also become more vulnerable to a virus or similar malware; therefore, it is essential that the networks are properly designed to avoid security breaches.

Schneier is critical of many of the modern security systems, for example, systems that use two-factor personal authentication. He finds personal authentication insufficient to provide real security because it does not account for a virus or other malware that can execute after a successful authentication took place. Instead of authenticating the person, these systems should aim to authenticate the transaction, similarly to how credit cards have been operating for many years. Schneier is also concerned that much of the post-9/11 world's obsession with security in practice translated into a shift in control by way of new IDs, government checks, no-fly lists, and other measures that in reality do not make us any more secure. He believes that a security system that is essentially a control system does not benefit security but instead leaves the system more vulnerable to a maliciously minded person who can falsely authenticate control permissions.

Schneier even offers himself as an example of how security should work. In an article in *Wired* magazine, he admits to running an open wireless network in his home. He sees no reason to encrypt it and does not consider encrypting it necessary in order to prevent unauthorized access to his computer. Instead, he

0011010100101001110101101010101011001010000

(continued from page 38)

repaired after the fact. It is only because of such defenses that banks, retailers, hospitals, and government agencies have become willing to make information inside their computer networks available for the public to access. As can be seen in the figure on page 38, an end user may access a corporate network using a laptop computer, running a Web browser and connecting to the corporate network

`100111010010101010011001011101101010100101001`

chooses to keep the computer itself secure, no matter what network it is on: his home network, the airport network, or the open wireless network in the neighborhood coffee shop, which he says poses a much greater risk to his computer than his open home network. Schneier limits his exposure to the security flaws of a particular network by increasing the security of the individual computer, thus removing the need to worry about the security of the network itself.

Schneier is also against the post-9/11 movement to create a national ID card in the United States (the REAL ID). He believes that the enhanced features of such a card will facilitate identity theft and jeopardize personal information and safety of many people who would not be required to provide it on a traditional driver's license, such as undercover police officers. An ID card, no matter how secure, will be forged, lost, stolen, and misused. The additional databases created to authenticate these national ID cards provide just another opportunity for a hacker to steal the information they contain. Besides, the size of the database, which must have information on every American and make it available to be accessed from airports, police cars, and other points, would make it an easy target for abuse and very difficult to keep secure. A single national ID card is a very valuable document with great incentives to forge it; hackers would be more tempted to forge it than any other document. Schneier believes that the increased costs associated with production of the IDs themselves as well as database creation and maintenance in the end will only result in increase of control by the federal government and interference with the way that individual states issue driver's licenses and not add any real security benefits to the general public. Schneier raises a similar issue with respect to the enhanced U.S. passports that come with a built-in microchip that is capable of contactless communication with a chip reader. He believes that it is an expensive and unnecessary measure that will make the documents more vulnerable to identity theft without providing any increased security.

`100111010010101010011001011101101010100101001`

through one or more internet service providers (ISPs), eventually leading to a router at the edge of the corporate network. The combinations of the router and all of the security mechanisms described above allows the end user to browse the company's Web site and engage in other online activities authorized by the company, without obtaining access to private information within the corporate network.

The increasing amount of sensitive information being stored within corporate and government networks that is now available for access online is imposing an increasingly high burden on the information technology (IT) managers who secure such networks. Even small slips in security for brief periods can expose the network to identity thieves and other criminals who can exploit the weakness to steal data. Such breaches can occur not only over the Internet but also within the walls of the company by employees who have direct physical access to the company's computers and can lead to invasions of privacy and financial harm to the people whose information is exposed. As a result, one could argue that IT managers have not only a legal obligation to their employers to maintain network security, but also an ethical obligation to the people in their employers' databases to protect the security of the network.

SOFTWARE SECURITY ISSUES AND PROGRAMMING ETHICS

Often, recently released computer software will contain a large number of bugs that can be exploited by viruses. For example, 27 bugs were reported in the six months after the release of Windows Vista in 2007, many of which were temporarily exploited by hackers to create malware. When a hacker exploits a software vulnerability, he or she can spread a malicious virus, or collect personal data. The most effective way to prevent these attacks is for the creator of the software to fix the bug and distribute an update, known as a patch, to the software's users. Once the bug is eliminated, the virus can no longer exploit it.

However, this raises the question whether software developers have any ethical responsibilities in connection with their handling of software bugs. For example, it is a common practice in the software industry to release software to the public even though the developers know that it contains bugs, including security flaws. Perhaps such a practice had no ethical implications in the early years of computers, when the presence of security flaws may have been an annoyance to users but did not carry the potential of causing substantial harm. Now, however, security flaws can lead to identity theft, actual monetary theft, and worse, so it is worth asking about the ethical responsibilities of software developers to eliminate all security flaws from their software before releasing it.

Even those who are not convinced by the ethical argument might be convinced by an economic argument: In 2003, CBS reported that software bugs cost the U.S. economy $59.5 billion. In their defense, software companies and developers argue that software is incredibly complex to create and that the cost of eradicating bugs, particularly obscure security-related bugs, is especially high. They claim that eliminating all such bugs would not only increase significantly the amount of time required to bring new products to market but also force them to increase the price of new software to cover the costs of bug-fixing. A software package that contained bugs and cost $49 might need to be sold for $149 if the software vendor needed to pay programmers for the additional time required to make the software bug-free. There is a case to be made that releasing low-priced software quickly with some bugs is better for the public than releasing high-priced software slowly without any bugs. At the very least, some argue that consumers of software are now sophisticated and should be allowed to make their own decisions about whether or not to buy a particular software package. Most who take this position, however, acknowledge that software vendors should make publicly available the full list of known bugs within each software package so that consumers can make informed choices about which software to buy.

Furthermore, many in the industry have attempted to lay out development protocols in response to the need for airtight security. In 2003, after Microsoft endured a host of major viruses, Bill Gates released a memo calling trustworthiness in computing the company's highest priority when developing new software. He identified the need for a platform dedicated to security that would make the user feel safe in all computing activities. In addition, several industry organizations, such as the *Association for Computing Machinery (ACM),* have created ethical codes designed to provide guidance for the industry. The ACM's *code of ethics* includes clauses such as the need for programmers to "Approve software only if they have a well-founded belief that it is safe, meets specifications, passes appropriate tests, and does not diminish quality of life, diminish privacy or harm the environment. The ultimate effect of the work should be to the public good." Despite these efforts, it is important to note that due to the nature of the computing industry, such as the fact that computer programmers in the United States are not required to obtain a professional license or sign a document agreeing to comply with the ACM's code of ethics, it is difficult to achieve strict regulation, making ethical dilemmas all the more complicated.

GOING PUBLIC WITH A SECURITY FLAW

As described above, computer software often contains bugs, and a bug in an important piece of software, such as an operating system, can create security risks. Such bugs often are not discovered until long after a piece of software has been released to the public and installed on many computers. In the case of fundamental software, such as an operating system, the software may already be relied upon to perform critical functions by government, corporations, universities, and individuals at the time the bug is discovered. The time immediately after such a discovery is made is a very critical and sensitive time, because it is a time when some people have gained knowledge of the bug and how to take advantage of it to evade security protections, and when computers containing the flawed software have not yet been protected against such attacks.

As a result, the person who discovers the bug is in a difficult ethical position. On one hand, the discoverer needs to share his or her newfound knowledge so that a patch for the bug can be developed and distributed. On the other hand, if knowledge of the bug is provided to too many people, or to the wrong people, before all computers can be patched, then such knowledge can be used to exploit the bug, such as by writing and distributing a virus to infect unprotected computers. Therefore, the bug's discoverer must carefully decide how, when, and to whom to reveal information about what the bug is and how it works.

Most software vendors argue that the solution to this problem is simple: The bug's discoverer should discreetly notify the software vendor of the bug and work with the vendor to develop a patch that can be distributed quickly and widely so that the bug can be fixed before it can be exploited for malicious purposes. Only after a patch has been developed and deployed should the bug's discoverer reveal information to the public at large.

As simple as this solution might seem, many security professionals argue that when they notify software companies of bugs in their software, their warnings fall on deaf ears; the software companies either take no action to fix the bug or take a very long time to solve the problem, even if the fix is simple. These security professionals claim that software vendors have little incentive to fix bugs that are not publicly known, because people do not complain to the software vendors about bugs that they do not know exist. Therefore, some argue that the best way to motivate software companies to fix bugs is to publish information about newly discovered bugs as widely as possible immediately after they are discovered, and

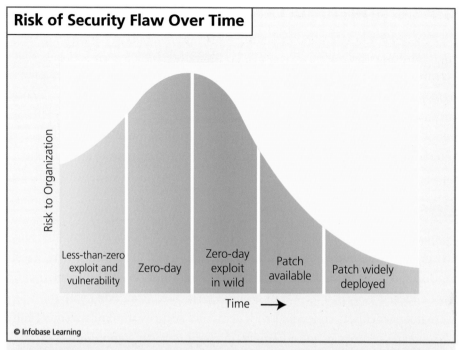

Risk of Security Flaw Over Time

Risk to Organization

Less-than-zero exploit and vulnerability   Zero-day   Zero-day exploit in wild   Patch available   Patch widely deployed

Time ⟶

© Infobase Learning

Security flaws that are known to hackers but not to the general public pose a risk of "less-than-zero day exploits," such as viruses launched to take advantage of the security flaw before the public knows that the flaw exists. Although such exploits are difficult to protect against, they are rare since the flaw is not widely known. The risk posed by security flaws is highest shortly after such flaws become known, because the number of people who know how to exploit the flaw is high, while the number of people who know how to protect against such exploits is low, and most computer systems have not yet been updated with protective patches. The risk posed then decreases over time as patches become available and are installed.

even to publish information about how to create viruses that exploit those bugs. This camp argues that only such action provides software vendors with the motivation to tackle and fix bugs quickly and effectively. In response, software companies argue that such widespread public disclosure harms the public by giving ammunition to the creators of malware and other criminals.

One solution to this dilemma is called *responsible disclosure.* Someone who discovers a software bug engages in responsible disclosure by informing the vendor of the flawed software that the bug exists and providing the vendor with some reasonable amount of time (e.g., 30 days) to correct the flaw. If the vendor does not fix the bug within the time limit, then the bug discoverer may reveal the bug to the public, allowing users to protect themselves against possible viruses. In 2004, the Organization for Internet Safety (OIS) issued a set of guidelines recommending this practice as a standard, and it has achieved some degree of agreement between security researchers and software vendors, serving as a compromise between immediate public disclosure and private disclosure to software vendors. However, in an industry that places a high value on the competing interests of freedom, access, and security, this issue continues to arouse debate.

CONCLUSIONS

Not long ago, computer security was a topic of concern only to computer security professionals employed by banks, universities, and the military. Even a generation ago, most private individuals stored their most sensitive information on paper, tucked away in a drawer or a safe-deposit box. Even avid computer users were not particularly concerned with computer security until relatively recently because the security of most computers could only be compromised through direct physical access. A complete personal computer security plan could consist solely of protecting one's computer against theft and locking access to it with a password.

Now it is difficult to use a computer for any extended period of time without issues of computer security intruding into one's consciousness and affecting one's actions. While logging in to a computer, most users are now careful no one is looking over their shoulder as they type their password. When downloading new e-mail, an automatic virus scanner displays an alert message indicating that an incoming message contains an attachment that has been infected with a known virus. When clicking on a link to a bank's Web site, a misspelling on the home page catches the user's attention, serving as a sign that the page has been hijacked for use in a phishing scam. Even a small slip of attention in any of these situations could lead to compromising one's own computer and possible exposure of one's personal data to an identity thief or theft of funds from a bank account. We must all be security-savvy computer users now.

Yet computer security is not solely an issue of self-protection. When the security of a computer is compromised, it can harm both the user whose actions lead to the breach and other users of the same computer—even users of other computers. Because ethics is concerned with an individual's responsibility not to harm others, the risks of computer security breaches now raise substantial ethical questions. Although clearly the person who creates or disseminates a computer virus has primary ethical responsibility for the harm the virus causes, this does not necessarily mean that the corporate IT department that fails to install antivirus software on the company's computers has no ethical responsibility for the theft of customer data that results from an infection of those computers.

The concept of negligence in tort law serves as a useful analogy. A person is considered negligent under the law if he or she has a duty toward a third party and the person fails to take reasonable precautions to prevent harm from coming to the third party in breach of that duty. For example, if a store owner accidentally spills grease on the store floor and fails to clean it up, leading to a customer slipping, falling, and injuring himself, then the store owner is liable for the customer's injuries. A reasonable store owner would have cleaned up the spill, and the store owner's failure to do so caused the customer's injury. Most would agree that the legal outcome in this situation is consistent with the conclusion that the storeowner is ethically responsible for the customer's fall.

In the early years of the computer industry, when little was known about computer security and the harm that could result from security violations, it may not have been reasonable to hold one person ethically responsible for harm to another person resulting from the first person's failure to sufficiently secure a computer. Yet, as understanding of the importance of computer security grows and as knowledge of steps for reliably maintaining security spreads, it is at least worth asking whether the relationship between all of us and our fellow computer users is increasingly coming to resemble that between the storeowner and customer from an ethical perspective.

3

ANONYMITY: ADVANTAGES AND DANGERS OF ANONYMOUS COMMUNICATION

Anonymity refers to interacting with others without revealing one's identity. Long before the creation of the Internet, it was possible to attain varying degrees of anonymity in certain situations. When attending confession, one might shield his or her identity from a priest or other religious leader. When reporting the results of a scientific study, the scientist could choose not to divulge the details of his or her participants. When placing a personal ad, one might use a pseudonym. In all of these examples, anonymity encourages people to speak and act freely without fear of negative repercussions. One reason that both children and adults enjoy Halloween is that it enables them to act playfully while anonymous and thereby avoid embarrassment in the eyes of their peers.

Internet technology has made it infinitely easier to achieve anonymity in a wide variety of circumstances. E-mail accounts and accounts on social networking sites can easily be created without providing one's real name, thereby enabling one to communicate with others anonymously. Similarly, one might create an avatar in a virtual world that bears no resemblance to one's appearance in the real world. Most blogs and other forums allow comments to be posted anonymously. Domain names can be purchased with protection against revealing oneself to the public as the owner of the domain name.

Savvy Internet users can trace e-mail messages back to their source with some effort. Similarly, Web site owners can track the *Internet Protocol (IP)* addresses of users who visit

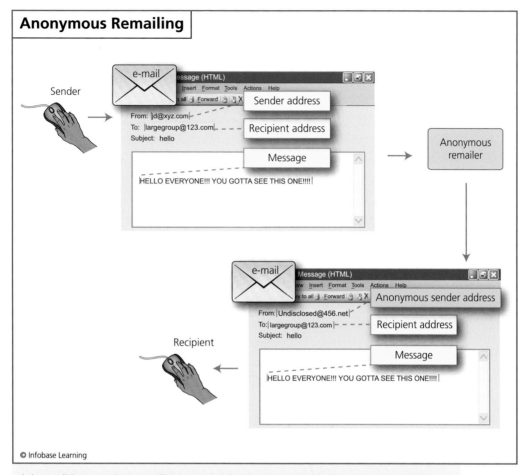

Anonymous Remailing

Sender

e-mail

...essage (HTML)

Insert Format Tools Actions Help

...p all Forward X

Sender address

From: |jd@xyz.com|

To: |largegroup@123.com|

Recipient address

Subject: hello

Message

|HELLO EVERYONE!!! YOU GOTTA SEE THIS ONE!!!!|

Anonymous remailer

e-mail

Message (HTML)

...ew Insert Format Tools Actions Help

...ly to all Forward X

Anonymous sender address

From: |Undisclosed@456.net|

To: |largegroup@123.com|

Recipient address

Subject: hello

Recipient

Message

|HELLO EVERYONE!!! YOU GOTTA SEE THIS ONE!!!!|

© Infobase Learning

It is possible to send an e-mail message while keeping one's identity secret by sending the e-mail message using an anonymous remailer, which strips out the sender's true e-mail address and replaces it with another, anonymous e-mail address, thereby making it impossible to trace the e-mail message back to the sender.

their sites. Those who desire extra protection against these and other mechanisms for unmasking their identity have a variety of options. Software, such as Anonymizer, can be purchased and installed on one's computer to prevent a Web site owner, or anyone else, from discovering which Web sites one has visited. Such software works by using a *proxy server*, which acts an as intermediary between the user who is browsing the Web and the Web site being visited. For example, if the user enters the address www.abc.com into the address bar, this address is intercepted by Anonymizer, which then downloads the home page of www.abc.com and forwards it back to the user. Because the user's Web browser never connects directly to www.abc.com, that Web site cannot detect the identity of the user. Instead, the Web site can only tell that it is being visited by Anonymizer's proxy server, which keeps no record of its users' Web browsing activity.

Similarly, e-mail messages can be transmitted anonymously using an anonymous remailer. Like software for making Web browsing anonymous, anonymous remailers also use a proxy server. When a user writes and transmits an e-mail message, the message is not transmitted directly to the recipient. Instead, it is transmitted to the anonymous remailer's proxy server, which replaces the sender's e-mail address with an anonymous e-mail address and then forwards the anonymous e-mail message to the recipient, who therefore never sees the sender's true e-mail address. Such an e-mail message, which does not contain the e-mail address or any other personally identifying information of the sender, is said to be *anonymized data* or *de-identified data.*

This chapter explores the potential benefits and harms of anonymity and considers the circumstances under which anonymity should be considered an ethical act and when one should be required to disclose one's identity in interactions with other people.

REGULATING ANONYMOUS SPEECH

While much of the Internet can still be navigated with relative anonymity, there are a number of situations in which Web sites attempt to regulate the use of anonymous personas, suggesting or requiring that users provide real personal information. These Web sites range from online banking systems to blogs, with a variety of different rationales for this practice. The ethical question, however, is whether any site should be able to require its visitors to disclose their true identities. To explore this question, consider the following examples.

Although the U.S. Supreme Court first decreed in *Buckley v. Valeo* that contributions to political campaigns are a kind of speech, those who make such contributions do not have a right to remain anonymous. Campaigns are required by law to publish financial disclosure reports, and many states are now enacting legislation that compels campaigns to publish these reports online. As campaigns, such as Barack Obama's in 2008, increasingly seek large numbers of small donations, such reports will reveal the identities of a larger number of donors to a greater online audience. During the 2008 presidential campaign, Obama adopted the online contribution methods of raising a large percentage of funds through small online individual donations popularized by Governor Howard Dean in his own run for the Democratic nomination.

There are many, however, who believe that anonymity should be protected within the contribution process. One argument is to encourage people to engage in the political process freely and openly without fear that they will be punished, ostracized, or discriminated against on the basis of their political views. Furthermore, they claim that any possible corrupting influence that campaign contributions might have on the political process could be guarded against simply by requiring candidates to disclose the number and amounts of contributions they receive, without disclosing the donors' identities. In addition, some campaign finance reform experts, such as Bruce Ackerman and Ian Ayres, authors of the landmark book *Voting with Dollars,* believe that all contributions should be made anonymously in order to lend more integrity to the political process. Were this system enacted, the Internet would be a perfect venue. Proponents of the current system, however, argue that anonymity could enable a small number of wealthy and powerful donors to wield undue influence over the political process by donating large sums of money to individual candidates to ensure their elections despite their unpopularity with the general public.

In January 2010, the U.S. Supreme Court, in a landmark decision, *Citizens United v. Federal Election Commission,* held that "A provision of the Bipartisan Campaign Reform Act prohibiting unions, corporations and not-for-profit organizations from broadcasting electioneering communications within 60 days of a general election or 30 days of a primary election violates the free speech clause of the First Amendment to the United States Constitution." This decision allowed corporations to spend unlimited money for candidates while avoiding disclosure.

Many business transactions that people use in their everyday life also prohibit anonymity. For instance, online banking systems are generally attached to

(continues on page 56)

00110101001010011101011010101010101011001010000l

WikiLeaks

In 2010, a series of secret military documents and videos were published on the Internet without the consent of the U.S. military. The leaks began in April with the release of video footage from an Apache helicopter cockpit showing U.S. air strikes that killed Iraqi civilians and two Reuters journalists. July saw the release of Afghan War Diary, a collection of more than 75,000 U.S. military reports related to the War in Afghanistan dating from 2004 to 2009. Then, in October, Iraq War Logs were released. This leak consisted of more than 390,000 individual reports on the War in Iraq, also dating from 2004 to 2009. These actions put focus on the secretive WikiLeaks organization, which made the information available to the *Guardian,* the *New York Times,* and *Der Spiegel,* and posted it on its Web site. Since its establishment in 2006, WikiLeaks has been controversial.

Few in the general public had heard of WikiLeaks before 2010. WikiLeaks is a nonprofit organization that uses a Web site to publish classified information that has been obtained from anonymous sources (also known as leaks). Like YouTube, WikiLeaks leverages the viral nature of the Internet to disseminate content that has been supplied by the public. The WikiLeaks Web site provides an electronic drop box mechanism that is based on cryptographic technology. This drop box allows a source to leak information without revealing his or her identity. In addition to the electronic drop box, information is also submitted to WikiLeaks through postal mail. Once a document, photograph, or video has been submitted to WikiLeaks, a team of volunteers investigates and analyzes it. When the investigative process is complete, a staff journalist writes a news story describing the significance of the leaked informa-

WikiLeaks founder Julian Assange leaves the Belmarsh Magistrates' Court in London to speak to the media after his extradition hearing in early 2011. *(AP Images)*

00110101001010011101011010101010101011001010000l

tion. The original document, image, or video is then released with the news story on the WikiLeaks Web site.

By hiding the identities of contributors, WikiLeaks protects whistle-blowers and activists who have made the decision to expose wrongdoing. Examples of other controversial material that has been posted on the WikiLeaks Web site include screenshots of presidential candidate Sarah Palin's e-mail inbox and address book, secret documents from the church of Scientology, diplomatic cables sent between U.S. embassies, and a copy of the operating manual for the U.S. prison camp at Guantánamo Bay in Cuba. It appears that WikiLeaks is putting stronger emphasis on balancing the exposure of government information with efforts to protect against the potential harm that could result from such exposure. For example, WikiLeaks redacted relatively little information from the set of documents that it released in 2010 in connection with the War in Afghanistan but redacted a much more significant amount from its release later in the same year of documents related to the war in Iraq.

The release of classified military documents by WikiLeaks in 2010 led many journalists to draw parallels with the Pentagon Papers case. In 1971, portions of a secret report created by the U.S. Department of Defense's Vietnam Study Task Force were leaked to the *New York Times* by a military analyst named Daniel Ellsberg. The report consisted of more than 7,000 pages in 47 volumes and had been classified as both Top Secret and Sensitive because its contents, if disclosed, would be an embarrassment to the Department of Defense and the U.S. government. Ellsberg's motivation in leaking the report was his opposition to the Vietnam War, which was still going on. Following publication of three excerpts from the report by the *New York Times,* President Richard M. Nixon and Attorney General John N. Mitchell obtained a federal injunction ordering the paper to cease publication of future articles related to the report. The *Times* appealed the injunction, causing it to be overturned quickly by the Supreme Court. The *Times* and the *Washington Post* then continued to publish articles on the Pentagon Papers. The information that was revealed had a major impact on Americans' perception of the Vietnam War and the Nixon administration. For the role he played as whistle-blower, Daniel Ellsberg was initially indicted for stealing secret documents and espionage. All charges were later dropped following a mistrial, but Ellsberg's life was forever altered by his decision to release the Pentagon Papers. In 2010, Assange was arrested for the alleged rape and molestation of two Swedish women. He is currently awaiting trial. If Ellsberg were faced with the same decision today, he would have the alternative of releasing the

(continues)

(continued)

A Redacted Document

The U.S. Military's primary focus needs to shift immediately from Iraq to Afghanistan, ████████████████████████████████ said Monday.

"We remain committed to █████████████████████████ But Afghanistan has been an economy of force operation for far too long," ███████████ ████████████████████████

████████ said he is "gravely concerned" about recent Taliban and al-Qaeda gains across much of southern Afghanistan and in Pakistan. "This isn't about 'can do' anymore. This is about 'must do,' ██ ██ ███████████████████████████████

████████ remarks came less than a week after the release of a State Department report indicating █████████████████████████ ██ terrorists, communicate with their followers, plot attacks and send fighters to support the insurgency in Afghanistan."

It noted that the largest number of attacks occurred in ████████████████ ████████████████████████████████████ where extremists have sought to challenge the government and extend Islamic law.

© Infobase Learning

Some of the text in a redacted document is blacked out, often using an indelible magic marker, to protect the identity of sources or to prevent other sensitive information from being revealed. Government agencies and officials often redact documents on the grounds that doing so is necessary to protect national security. In some cases, so much text is redacted that the meaning of the original text can be lost. When redacted documents are provided by one party to another in a lawsuit, the receiving party may complain that too much information has been redacted, thereby requiring the judge to make a decision about whether to require some of the redacted text to be revealed.

documents through WikiLeaks and avoiding personal involvement and prosecution. However, Julian Assange, the editor in chief of WikiLeaks, has been hounded by Western governments, accused of personal misdeeds, and threatened with criminal investigation by Eric Holder, the U.S. attorney general. In fact, Daniel Ellsberg has stated: "Every attack against Assange and @ Wikileaks (the WikiLeaks Twitter hashtag) was also made against me and release of the Pentagon Papers."

Due to the use of Wiki, many have assumed that WikiLeaks is related to the Wikimedia Foundation (publisher of the Wikipedia Web site). This is not the case. WikiLeaks is an independent organization without affiliations. The WikiLeaks Web site describes the organization's founders as "Chinese dissidents, journalists, mathematicians and start-up company technologists, from the U.S., Taiwan, Europe, Australia and South Africa." Like its sources, the WikiLeaks staff is for the most part anonymous. An Australian activist named Julian Assange is the most visible representative of the organization. According to Assange, hundreds of volunteers maintain the WikiLeaks Web site and work as journalists and editors for the organization. The organization's database of information currently contains more than 1 million items. This information is contained on multiple computer servers located in several different countries.

Critics of WikiLeaks say the site poses a risk to national security and endangers the safety and livelihoods of innocent people. U.S. intelligence agencies have called WikiLeaks a "threat to the U.S. Army." (This statement came from a classified document released on WikiLeaks in March 2010.) Private Bradley Manning, the soldier who allegedly leaked classified documents pertaining to the Iraq War and more than 250,000 diplomatic cables, was arrested in May 2010 and charged with treason. WikiLeaks has recognized these concerns and other ethical issues related to the disclosure of classified material. Although WikiLeaks does not have a censorship policy, the organization will delay or stop publication of material that it deems to be a threat to the safety of innocent people.

Supporters of WikiLeaks hope that the Web site will usher in a new era of government and corporate transparency. Some see it as the future of investigative journalism. WikiLeaks has been the recipient of several awards, including the New Media awards from *Economist* magazine and Amnesty International. In 2010, the *New York Daily News* put WikiLeaks at the top of a list of Web sites that have the potential to radically transform how news is disseminated.

(continued from page 51)

a user's offline account, created through legitimate channels in which the user's true name is verified. Even PayPal, the online transaction Web site, requires verifiable personal information to create an account. The most common ethical justification for prohibiting anonymity in banking is that to allow anonymity would facilitate a wide variety of criminal activity, which is already difficult to detect and prosecute.

Critics argue that the economy needs to retain some ability for people to engage in anonymous transactions to maintain the privacy of sensitive purchases, such as politically unpopular books or birth control products. They point to the fact that anonymity in financial transactions was the norm throughout most of history, when cash was widely used and credit cards and online accounts did not exist. Even if there is good reason to prohibit anonymity in certain kinds of financial transactions, it is worth thinking carefully about whether some room needs to be left open for anonymous transactions even in a world in which most or all transactions are conducted electronically.

Another example of anonymous behavior is posting to blogs. While many blogs do allow the input of anonymous members, a large number have instituted protections against such practices, citing instances of *spam,* scams, and unruly participants. In 2006, in the *Online Journalism Review,* Vin Crosbie advocated for these kinds of safeguards, suggesting that in public journalistic discourse readers should not demand a greater level of anonymity than is afforded to the writers themselves. Others, however, believe that anonymity can provide individuals with the ability to contribute more openly and honestly to discussions, particularly in the case of people who are shy or whose contributions might lead to embarrassment or ridicule.

Interestingly, while the Internet provides a forum for anonymous communication, users often find that operating under real names affords them more respect and legitimacy. For example, under Amazon.com's Real Name program, users can elect to use their legal names when posting reviews, operating under the assumption that other users will be more likely to trust the opinions of those who are willing to share their names. If this assumption is correct and anonymity carries with it a stigma of untrustworthiness, then perhaps the desire to avoid criticism will limit the extent to which people use and abuse anonymity online.

ANONYMITY, CONFIDENTIALITY, AND WHISTLE-BLOWING

As long as there have been corruption and misconduct, there have been whistle-blowers. Whether seen as martyrs or tattletales, they are the individuals who sound the alarm on bad behavior, either within a company, a government, or some other organization. *Internal whistle-blowers* are those who uncover misconduct within their own workplace; *external whistle-blowers* exist outside an organization, i.e., the media. Famous whistle-blowers include Jeffrey Wigand of Brown & Williamson, Sherron Watkins of Enron, and "Deep Throat," Mark Felt, an informant who revealed information about President Nixon's illegal activities.

Whistle-blowing in general, especially internal whistle-blowing, raises serious ethical questions. While some believe that whistle-blowers are following an ethical imperative by protecting the public from the harmful misconduct of companies and organizations, others warn that would-be whistle-blowers might use this tactic to *slander* those against whom they may harbor personal grudges, exposing proprietary information as they do so. In this case, opponents of whistle-blowing argue that the practice is ethically negligent. Information revealed through whistle-blowing, especially in a government context, could be potentially harmful and those who are slandered could lose their reputations, careers, or lives.

Currently, there are new legal protections for whistle-blowers in the United States, effective March 23, 2010. In §1558 of the Affordable Care Act (ACA) of 2010, employees are protected against discrimination for whistle-blowing. The Occupational Safely and Health Administration (OSHA) has an Office of the Whistleblower Protection Program and has published a fact sheet concerning your rights as a whistle-blower (http://63.234.227.130/OshDoc/data_General_Facts/whistleblower_rights.pdf).

Ethical questions surrounding whistle-blowing become more complicated in connection with anonymous whistle-blowing. Some argue that whistle-blowers should be allowed to remain anonymous in order to provide them with greater protection against possible retaliation and other consequences of whistle-blowing. The strongest argument in favor of protecting the anonymity of whistle-blowers is that they often speak out against corporations, governments, and other entities that have the power to ruin lives. Without the protection of anonymity, few people would take the personal risk required to be a whistle-

(continues on page 60)

Personal Cost of Whistle-blowing

Throughout the years, many whistle-blowers have endured various consequences based on their choice to come forward, both positive and negative. The following are a few of their stories.

The classic whistle-blower is Daniel Ellsberg, the former U.S. military analyst who released the Pentagon Papers (which provided embarrassing and incriminating evidence regarding the government's knowledge about the Vietnam War) to the *New York Times* in 1971. Following the leak, the Nixon administration targeted Ellsberg personally, engaging in a number of criminal activities, including burglary and wiretapping. Ellsberg was placed on trial for leaking the information. However, due to the government's extreme misconduct, he was allowed to walk free. Although at the time Ellsberg risked being found guilty of treason, in retrospect his actions have been vindicated and his reputation bolstered in the eyes of the public.

In 1972, FBI official Mark Felt served as the anonymous whistle-blower *Deep Throat* during the Watergate scandal. After serving as the source for *Washington Post* reporters Bob Woodward and Carl Bernstein, Felt denied his involvement for 30 years, only coming clean in 2005. Although he might have suffered serious consequences if he had revealed his true identity during the heat of the Watergate scandal, by waiting more than 30 years he largely escaped the kind of scandal that typically surrounds whistle-blowers.

Karen Silkwood is one of the best known whistle-blowers due to her death under mysterious circumstances. Her life story was made into *Silkwood,* a 1983 film starring Meryl Streep and Cher and directed by Mike Nichols. Silkwood worked at a nuclear power plant in Oklahoma, making plutonium pellets for nuclear reactor fuel rods. After being elected to her union's bargaining committee, she claimed to have uncovered the exposure of power plant workers to nuclear contamination, among other health and safety violations. As a representative of the union, she testified to the Atomic Energy Commission (AEC) about these problems. Soon after, she tested positive for plutonium contamination several times and later died when her car ran off the road. Significant controversy remains to this day over whether her contamination and death were the result of foul play directed at squelching her public criticism of her employer.

1001110100101010100110010111011010100101001

In 2001, Sibel Edmonds was hired as an interpreter in the translations unit of the FBI. However, after just a few months, Edmonds began to notice suspicious activity, including the presence of corruption and foreign intelligence networks. In addition, she claimed to find evidence that the FBI had received intelligence about potential terrorism prior to 9/11. She reported her observations to her superiors. Then, in March 2002, she was fired, and her court testimony was blocked by the state secrets privilege, which enables evidence to be excluded from court if the government submits affidavits indicating that such evidence might endanger national security.

Karen Silkwood, a whistle-blower in the nuclear power industry whose untimely death remains clouded in controversy *(AP Images)*

In 2004, Sergeant Joseph Darby acted as a whistle-blower in the Abu Ghraib torture scandal, exposing the abuse of detainees by U.S. military personnel. Although Darby initially asked to remain anonymous, Donald Rumsfeld disclosed his name during a Senate hearing. After his identity had been revealed, the press celebrated Darby's actions. However, some were not so receptive to what the media called heroism. In Darby's community in Maryland, neighbors shunned him and his wife, forcing them to go into protective custody.

In 2005, Shawn Carpenter was an employee of Sandia National Laboratories who had been hired to investigate security breaches. After completing a thorough investigation of the security history, however, Carpenter uncovered a Chinese cyber-espionage scheme code-named Titan Rain by the FBI. After reporting his findings to his superiors, Carpenter was told to keep quiet about Titan Rain's attacks. Carpenter disobeyed his employers, instead serving as an informant for the FBI. After learning of this, Sandia officials fired Carpenter. Eventually, he received $4.7 million in damages in a 2007 trial.

1001110100101010100110010111011010100101001

(continued from page 57)
blower. Others believe that tolerating anonymity only increases the chance that disgruntled employees will make slanderous and untruthful accusations against their employers and it is necessary to require whistle-blowers to reveal their true identities in order to keep them honest. Some companies, such as Crime Stoppers, market an anonymous hotline to companies that serves as a method for employees to register complaints against their employers without fear or retaliation. With the Internet, the potential for anonymous whistle-blowing has only grown.

ANONYMOUS SPEECH AND NEWS REPORTING

Just as the debate continues over whether whistle-blowers should be allowed to remain anonymous, a similar question arises in connection with news reporters and their sources. In terms of the journalists themselves, little tradition exists when it comes to anonymous journalism. While many famous figures, including John Adams, Benjamin Franklin, and Alexander Hamilton, published under pseudonyms, virtually no reputable newspapers have made it a policy to publish material by writers whose identities were entirely unknown to them. Although modern publications such as the *Economist* frequently print material that does not include bylines, there is a general understanding that such material has been written by authors who are known to the publication's editors and who therefore are not entirely anonymous. The primary reason for requiring the authors to be known, at least to the publisher, is to ensure writing quality and to protect against individuals using newspapers as vehicles for personal vendettas.

With the Internet, the potential for truly anonymous journalism has emerged. Either through personal news blogs or user-submitted content to other online sources, anyone can now voice an opinion to a wide audience without being required to share his or her real name or identity with anyone. As such, the ethical question emerges whether it is right for Internet users to publish news or opinion anonymously. On one hand, the veracity of sources and material cannot easily be verified if authors submit content without identifying themselves, which would argue in favor of requiring all articles and other news-related postings on the Internet to carry the true name of the author. On the other hand, there is some reason to allow those who post sensitive information to retain

(continues on page 64)

`1001110100101010101001100101110110101001011001`

Alexander Hamilton, James Madison, and John Jay *(Publius)*

Alexander Hamilton was born in Charlestown, on the island of Nevis in the British West Indies on January 11, 1757, immigrated to the United States in 1772, and studied at what is now Columbia University in New York City. He joined the Continental army in New York in 1776 as an artillery captain and was appointed an aide-de-camp to General George Washington, a position in which he served from March 1777 to February 1781. He was elected to the Continental Congress and served in the New York State assembly in 1778. He was appointed as the first Secretary of the Treasury at the inauguration of the first constitutional government in 1789.

As the first secretary, Hamilton had a great deal of influence over how the Treasury Department functioned. He frequently battled with Thomas Jefferson, the secretary of state, and Albert Gallatin, a congressman, over how much power the department should have. Hamilton envisioned a strong, centrally controlled Treasury, which he designed to promote the economic development of the nation as well as collection and disbursement of public revenue.

Hamilton's first goal as secretary was to repay the war debt in full, thus signaling to the foreign powers that the United States was a responsible nation worthy of their confidence. He established the First Bank of the United States in 1791. The bank served as a depository of public funds and as a financial agent of the Treasury Department and issued paper currency. Hamilton also established the United States Mint, which was initially created under the State Department in 1792 under pressure from Jefferson, but eventually transferred to the Treasury in 1873. In 1795, under great financial strain, Hamilton resigned his $3,500 a year office and returned to the practice of law as a member of the New York bar. He was killed in a duel with Aaron Burr in 1804 following a political debate.

James Madison, the fourth president of the United States, was born in 1751 in Orange County, Virginia, into a family of tobacco plantation owners. He attended Princeton, then known as the College of New Jersey. Well-read in history, government, and law, Madison served in the Continental Congress and led the Virginia assembly. He took part in the Constitutional Convention in Philadelphia,

(continues)

`1001110100101010101001100101110110101001011001`

```
00110101001010011010110101010101100101000001
```

(continued)

and, as a member of Congress, was a key contributor to the writing of the Bill of Rights. His opposition to the financial plans of Treasury secretary Hamilton resulted in creation of the Republican (Jeffersonian) Party, which became the party of the common man, advancing the interests of the population that Jefferson considered to be the foundation of the nation. Madison served as President Jefferson's secretary of state and was one of the key figures behind the Embargo Act of 1807, which contributed to a severe economic depression and was soon repealed.

Madison was elected president of the United States in 1808. During his presidency, the United States declared war on Britain. The small and unprepared American army suffered a crushing defeat, and the British invaded Washington. Madison retired to his estate in Virginia after completing his second term as president. Together with Jefferson, he worked on establishing the University of Virginia, which under their care soon became one of the premier educational institutions in the country. Both Madison and Jefferson were personally involved in writing the curriculum, attracting the best teachers, and employing the most effective teaching methods.

> ### THE
> # FEDERALIST:
> #### ADDRESSED TO THE
> ## PEOPLE OF THE STATE OF NEW-YORK.
>
> ---
>
> #### NUMBER I.
>
> *Introduction.*
>
> AFTER an unequivocal experience of the inefficacy of the subsisting federal government, you are called upon to deliberate on a new constitution for the United States of America. The subject speaks its own importance; comprehending in its consequences, nothing less than the existence of the UNION, the safety and welfare of the parts of which it is composed, the fate of an empire, in many respects, the most interesting in the world. It has been frequently remarked, that it seems to have been reserved to the people of this country, by their conduct and example, to decide the important question, whether societies of men are really capable or not, of establishing good government from reflection and choice, or whether they are forever destined to depend, for their political constitutions, on accident and force. If there be any truth in the remark, the crisis, at which we are arrived, may with propriety be regarded as the æra in which
>
> A   that

Alexander Hamilton, James Madison, and John Jay wrote *The Federalist* (known now as *The Federalist Papers*) shortly after the formation of the United States to advocate for the adoption of the United States Constitution. They used the pseudonym "Publius" to protect their identities, which remained secret until after Hamilton's death.   *(North Wind Picture Archives/Alamy)*

```
00110101001010011010110101010101100101000001
```

Madison continued to correspond with important political figures in the country long after his retirement and frequently entertained guests at his Virginia home. He died on June 28, 1836.

John Jay was born on December 12, 1745, in New York City, and grew up in Rye, New York. He graduated from what is now Columbia University in 1764 and became a clerk in the law firm of Benjamin Kissam. Jay was admitted to the New York bar in 1786 and opened his own law office in 1771. Jay's marriage to Sarah Livingston, the daughter of New Jersey governor William Livingston, propelled him into the political arena. Jay served as the delegate to both the First and Second Continental Congresses and became the chief justice of the New York Supreme Court before being elected president of the Continental Congress in 1778.

President Washington appointed Jay as the first chief justice of the United States Supreme Court in 1789. During his time on the bench, Jay advanced his nationalist views. His opinion in the case of *Chisholm v. Georgia* motivated the adoption of the Eleventh Amendment, which protects states' rights. In 1794, he was chosen by Washington to negotiate a treaty with Great Britain in order to resolve lingering issues between the two nations. The Jay Treaty was very controversial and unpopular and contributed to the growth of opposition to the Federalists.

In 1795, John Jay was elected to the New York State governorship, a position that he previously unsuccessfully sought. He served two terms in this post and eventually retired from public life in 1801. He died on May 17, 1829, at the age of 83.

Hamilton, Madison, and Jay were the unattributed authors of *The Federalist Papers,* originally titled *The Federalist.* These papers consisted of 85 essays that advocated the ratification of the United States Constitution and remain today a primary source in interpreting the founders' philosophies and motivations.

In order to avoid the ill effects of association, *The Federalist* was published anonymously. Hamilton, Madison, and Jay chose "Publius" as a pseudonym to honor the Roman consul Publius Valerius Publicola, a leader in the founding of the Roman Republic.

These essays appeared in three New York newspapers and were reprinted in several other states. Although no one can prove they affected the ratification of the Constitution, their effect on history has been enormous. From their inception to today, scholars and schoolchildren study them to understand the great minds behind the founding of the United States.

(continued from page 60)
their secret identity to avoid retaliation. In other words, as the Internet gives individuals the ability to disseminate news and opinion to a wide audience, some of the ethical considerations that traditionally have applied to whistle-blowers now arguably apply to individuals posting information on the Internet.

In addition to this issue, there is the separate question of whether it is ethical for journalists and other authors to use anonymous sources, i.e., to provide information in news articles that was obtained from people whose names are not revealed in the news article itself. Most news organizations use anonymous sources, if the sources are known to be reliable by the journalist, if the source has special knowledge of a topic of interest to the public, and if the source would be unwilling to speak without the promise of anonymity. In these situations, the use of anonymous sources enables the public to obtain information, often about the government, that it would be unable to obtain otherwise. However, the overuse of anonymous sources can lead to misinformation and scandal, as was seen in cases of journalists who fabricated stories without any real sources at all. Some news organizations have attempted to achieve balance by enforcing policies about anonymous sources more consistently and by hiring people whose job is to police the ethical conduct of the reporters and others within the organization. However, internal oversight always runs the risk of being biased in favor of the organization itself. Although such efforts are admirable, in the end the right balance will always require an informed and attentive public able to read and think critically and to hold journalists accountable when they use anonymous sources irresponsibly.

CONCLUSIONS

Clearly, anonymity on the Internet can provide many benefits, such as the opportunity to discuss sensitive matters without fear of exposure or embarrassment or the ability to protect one's personal information. However, anonymity can also be harmful. For example, anonymity can be used to engage in criminal activity without detection or to seek out unsuspecting victims for fraud, theft, and other malicious purposes. Furthermore, anonymity can be used as a cloak behind which one can slander or otherwise harm others without fear of repercussions.

To address these negative aspects of anonymity on the Internet, some technology is now available for verifying users' identities before they post information online. For example, many blogs and other online forums now require those who wish to post comments to first provide information about their real identities. Some social networking sites, such as LinkedIn, also require registered users to verify their identities before communicating with other members.

Furthermore, an increasing number of Web sites now use *CAPTCHAs*— short tests to ensure that a user is human—to prevent comments from being posted and other actions from being taken by software. Although CAPTCHAs can only distinguish humans from computers, not one human from another, they at least protect against the kind of wholesale copying of information that

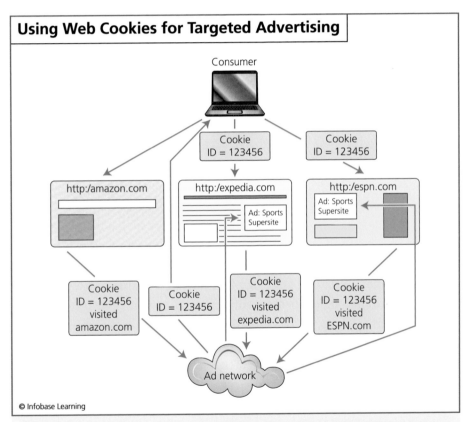

Using Web Cookies for Targeted Advertising

Consumer

Cookie
ID = 123456

Cookie
ID = 123456

http:/amazon.com

http:/expedia.com

Ad: Sports
Supersite

http:/espn.com

Ad: Sports
Supersite

Cookie
ID = 123456
visited
amazon.com

Cookie
ID = 123456

Cookie
ID = 123456
visited
expedia.com

Cookie
ID = 123456
visited
ESPN.com

Ad network

© Infobase Learning

Web sites use sets of data called cookies to keep track of information about people who visit their sites. One way in which cookies are used is to display advertisements that are targeted to the user, based on the user's previous purchases, even if purchases were made on a different Web site from the one currently being viewed. Some users may not be aware that their online purchases are being tracked and used to generate targeted advertisements in this way.

can be used to spread rumors and other falsehoods more quickly than any human could hope to do.

Perhaps the strongest protection against abuses of anonymity is the growing extent to which technologies for tracking the online activities of users are making it increasingly difficult for all but the most technically savvy users to remain anonymous. Even in the earliest days of the Web, *cookies* were used by Web sites to track which pages users visited, which products they purchased, and which advertisements they clicked on. In recent years, Web sites, advertisers, software vendors, and other parties have created highly sophisticated software tools for tracking nearly every aspect of users' online activity, often without users' knowledge. For example, a site such as Facebook allows application developers to access user details, including names, addresses, and telephone numbers, and to use such information in the applications they write.

A recent study by the *Wall Street Journal* found that the 50 most visited sites on the Web install a total of 3,180 tracking tools on the computers of those who visit them. Some individual sites install more than 100 tracking tools just by visiting the site. Some of these tools gathered such a wide variety of data from users' computers that they enabled data-gathering companies to identify the age, gender, race, zip code, income, marital status, health concerns, recent purchases, and favorite TV shows and movies of Web site visitors. Although most sites claim to use this data solely to learn more about their customers so that they can provide targeted advertising and create content that is better suited to their readers, there are few restrictions on what companies can do with such data once it is obtained.

Most computer users are not aware that such data are being gathered about them. Furthermore, although most antivirus and computer security software can block such tracking, many users do not have such software installed or properly configured, and some security software must be specially configured to block cookies and other tracking tools that are often considered low-level threats in comparison to viruses and Trojan horses. Therefore, even users who have installed security software and keep it up to date may not be protected against the latest tools for conducting online surveillance.

Therefore, although anonymity was the general rule at the birth of the World Wide Web, it is quickly becoming the exception. As a result, fears over the abuse of anonymity may soon need to take a backseat to concern over how to remain anonymous in the face of an increasing array of businesses and technologies whose aim is to uncover the identities of everyone who surfs the Web.

4

VIRTUAL WORLDS: LIVING INSIDE YOUR COMPUTER

In its most general sense, a *virtual world* is any computer simulation that provides users with the illusion of interacting with a real or fictional environment. Although some virtual worlds allow multiple people, connected to each other over the Internet or other network, to interact within the virtual world, some virtual worlds enable a single person to explore even in the absence of other users. These worlds, however, often include computer-simulated characters with whom the human user may interact. Many virtual worlds allow a combination of multiple human users and multiple computer-simulated characters to interact.

Users have inhabited virtual worlds since the earliest days of computers and the Internet. The exact character of these worlds, however, has changed significantly over time. Some early virtual worlds, such as *multi-user domains (MUD)* were purely text-based. MUDs described the environment to users using text, enabling users to imagine the contents of the world, much as if reading a book. Users then engaged in actions within the virtual world by typing commands, such as "look up," "turn right," or "run." Similarly, many early adventure games, such as Zork, Enchanter, and Planetfall, used purely textual interfaces.

Soon, however, programmers became interested in applying graphics and 3-D technology to these new virtual spaces, creating early versions of what we now recognize as virtual worlds (such as the graphical chat platform WorldsAway and Cityspace, an educational 3-D environment for children). Today, virtual worlds have become increasingly more sophisticated. Some exist as commercial multiplayer games oriented around a particular fictional storyline, such as World of Warcraft. Others are more social spaces that developed directly from the earlier text-based environments and allow users to interact using alternate identities, often in a role-playing situation. Some of these social environments

A Virtual World

© Infobase Learning

Virtual worlds often take the form of games in which players are represented by avatars with special powers. Although early virtual worlds consisted solely of text and therefore resembled interactive books, today's virtual worlds typically use three-dimensional animation to produce lifelike scenes.

also exist as idealized versions of reality, such as the Sims Online or Second Life. Often, users are able to build virtual homes, families, businesses, and more. In addition to social interaction, these build-your-own spaces are now being used for education and training in various fields. Companies have also attempted to capitalize on these new environments by using the virtual world technology for marketing and entertainment purposes.

Even when such virtual worlds are used for entertainment, they often do not involve accumulating scores, defeating enemies, or solving puzzles. Furthermore, it is not possible to win in a virtual world such as the Sims or Second Life. Therefore, such virtual worlds differ from those that are intended to serve purely as video games.

As virtual world technology becomes more and more complex, it can often be difficult to determine where the real world ends and the virtual world begins.

What follows is a more detailed exploration of virtual worlds and the ethical and philosophical dilemmas surrounding them.

TECHNOLOGY BEHIND VIRTUAL WORLDS

Today's virtual worlds depend on a variety of advanced technologies. Fortunately for software developers, much of this technology is becoming increasingly available at low cost to a wide variety of users. One particularly ubiquitous technological innovation that enables highly realistic virtual worlds inhabited by large numbers of users is the low-cost, high-speed Internet connection. Virtual worlds are particularly dependent on such connections because their 3-D animated graphical user interfaces require large volumes of data to be transmitted to the user very quickly to sustain the illusion that the user is immersed in a realistic world. Even short delays in transmitting audio or video to the user can break the illusion and cause users to become frustrated and unable to interact with each other and the virtual environment realistically. In July 2009, the Internet infrastructure company Akamai reported that broadband usage had grown worldwide, with the average connection speed rising 15 percent in the United States in only one year. This development has boosted the popularity of virtual worlds because it has both enabled the creation of more realistic simulated environments and a larger number and more diverse set of users to join virtual worlds. No one wants to enter a virtual world with few participants, and the richness of the simulated experience grows as the number and variety of participants grows. Therefore, virtual worlds are likely to become both more popular and more complex as high-speed Internet connections grow ever faster and less expensive.

In addition, virtual worlds rely on *video cards,* also known as *graphics accelerator cards,* to render 3-D imagery that delivers a realistic experience to the user. Although in the 1980s some early virtual worlds used 2-D video cards, in 1995, 3-D functions became more fully incorporated into the typical home computer. Now, 3-D video cards designed and manufactured by companies such as nVidia and ATI are used in most major personal computers and game consoles. Typically, the graphics accelerator card in a home computer is significantly more powerful than the computer's main processor, the central processing unit (CPU). To understand just how fast today's video cards are, consider that such cards create the illusion of a 3-D scene by displaying objects constructed out of very small triangles and other polygons. Such polygons are so small that they are not visible to the human eye (and may even constitute a single pixel on the screen) and therefore blend with each other to create a scene that appears similar to a photograph of a real environment. Furthermore, the video card can fill each polygon or other region on the screen with a texture, such as a pattern resembling stone, fabric, or wood, to add further realism. The most powerful graphics accelerator cards available as of this writing were capable of filling almost 50 billion on-screen polygons with textures per second. As a result, video cards are now capable of providing increasingly realistic simulations of complex phenomena such as flowing water, smoke, and fire.

Large virtual worlds inhabited by thousands or millions of users roaming through the world simultaneously require large numbers of computers to continuously perform the calculations necessary to update the world many times per second in response to input from users and other changes within the simulated environment. To satisfy this demand, companies that host virtual worlds take advantage of *server farms,* which are large clusters of computers connected to each other so that they operate as if they are a single very large computer. Fortunately for providers and users of virtual worlds, server farm technology has developed rapidly since the 1990s in response to the need for large Web sites. Therefore, virtual worlds have been able to piggyback on such developments to keep pace with the growing demands of virtual worlds.

Finally, virtual environments only appear to be realistic if objects move through space in ways that comply with the laws of physics. Therefore, programmers who create and maintain virtual worlds use physics engines to simulate people walking, planes flying, firing burning, water flowing, and other phenomena. Physics engines have grown increasingly realistic in the last few decades as a result of their development for use in video games and military training. Therefore, once again, virtual worlds have been able to take advantage of technological developments in other fields to improve the experience of virtual world users.

SECOND LIFE

In 1999, Philip Rosedale created Linden Lab, a group that focused on developing hardware for virtual reality experiences. After failing to produce a successful prototype, the Linden Lab developers transitioned into the realm of software, creating what would eventually become the popular virtual world application Second Life. By September 2008, more than 15 million accounts were registered in the Second Life database.

At its core, Second Life allows users *(residents)* to create alternate identities for themselves and interact with others in a virtual version of real life. Users can build within the world, buy and sell goods, and generally create their own alternate reality. The world operates using its own currency, the Linden dollar, which governs all *inworld* transactions. In addition, users who buy premium accounts can own property within Second Life.

Although Second Life's primary population consists of individuals who engage in virtual social activities, many businesses and organizations have attempted to capitalize on Second Life's popularity. Some universities, colleges, schools, and for-profit companies have begun using the Second Life platform for educational purposes, delivering inworld content related to subjects such as

(continues on page 74)

The Second Life virtual world includes many destinations that mirror those in the real world such as shopping malls, private homes, and public parks. Users can purchase products and exchange items with each other within Second Life. *(AP Images)*

001101010010101001110101101010101011001010000 1

Philip Rosedale (Creator of Online World "Second Life")

Philip Rosedale, born in 1968, developed an interest in virtual reality and computer technology as a child, building his first computer in fourth grade and programming computers as early as junior high school. At 17, he started a company installing computer systems for local businesses. He used the proceeds to pay for his college education, earning a bachelor's degree in physics from the University of California at San Diego.

After graduating from college in 1994, Rosedale moved to the San Francisco Bay Area. Although he briefly entertained the idea of a virtual world then, he concluded that in order to be successful, a virtual reality has to be similar to the world of video gaming. The relatively young field of computer graphics made it impossible to do 3-D simulations on a personal computer, and so instead Rosedale worked on a video compression algorithm that made it possible to compress video so that it could be streamed live on a computer connected to the Internet. This videoconferencing system was called FreeVue and caught the eye of Rob Glaser, whose RealNetworks purchased FreeVue in 1996. Glaser offered Rosedale a position at RealNetworks. Waiting for the virtual reality field to mature so that he could pursue his original project, Rosedale accepted, hoping to use his new position to obtain engineering management experience. He stayed for three years and became the chief technology officer. In 1999, Rosedale returned to San Francisco and started

Philip Rosedale, creator of the Second Life virtual world   *(Patrick Kovarik/ AFP/Getty Images)*

001101010010101001110101101010101011001010000 1

1001110100010101010011000101110110101001011001

his own company, Linden Lab, named after Linden Alley in Hayes Valley, where the company's office was located.

Rosedale had a clear vision for Second Life. He wanted to create a complex system that supported user-created content that would allow the system to be modified by the game participants themselves and would allow participants to be entrepreneurial if they so chose. The system was to run as a live 3-D environment, in which people could work, play, and function very much as they do in real life. However, the project was met with significant skepticism, as most people did not think it could recoup the money spent on it and that the idea was impossible to implement. Rosedale invested about a million dollars of his own money, and others also invested, who were most likely investing in him rather than the Second Life project, hoping that the smart young man could somehow figure out how to make the company a success.

The biggest concern of Second Life skeptics was the need for user-created content, such as homes, stores, and clothing, and whether large numbers of people would be willing to put in the effort needed to generate it without being paid. At the time, all computer graphics applications were top-down creations: A designer came up with the idea and created the content, and users were mere visitors into the already-created world. The original response to the idea of user-created content was lukewarm and caused some confusion. Six long years passed, during which Linden Lab and Second Life received very little publicity, and Rosedale was continuously pressured to make his virtual world more like a conventional video game. Lack of support caused financial hardships, which resulted in a third of the 30-person firm being laid off in 2003.

Recognizing that a few people were putting a lot of effort into building user-created content, Rosedale opened the entrepreneurial element of the game even further by allowing users to claim copyright protection on their creations within Second Life. As a result, Second Life truly became a real world that had an economy, where land was valuable and could be bought and sold and in which money could be earned. This attracted both significant attention and new investors, and by 2005, Second Life was beginning to gather momentum and a sizeable following. People were holding business meetings in Second Life. As of November 2010, Second Life had more than 21.3 million accounts registered. Today's users of Second Life are more diverse than the original technologically savvy group.

(continues)

1001110100010101010011000101110110101001011001

(continued)

Linden Lab continues working on making the service easier to use, especially for the casual user, hoping that more people will join as it becomes friendlier and easier to operate.

Second Life has been successful in spite of some competition from other virtual worlds, or *metaverses,* such as Google's Lively. Although Google shut down Lively at the end of 2008 due to lackluster response, Second Life remains profitable and growing. Rosedale believes that the relative lack of success of other virtual worlds does not invalidate the segment's viability but is merely an indication that much more work is needed in order for virtual worlds to become widely successful. He also continues to stress that the ability of people to create their own content and make money from it is what keeps Second Life successful over the competition. Linden Lab is currently working with IBM and other companies on standardizing virtual worlds and making them interoperable.

Rosedale's emphasis on entrepreneurship is visible in the way that Linden Lab is organized. It purposefully lacks centralization, instead focusing on individual creativity to drive the business process. However, with the company growing to more than 300 employees in 2008, it is uncertain whether the decentralized model will remain in place. Rosedale resigned as CEO of Linden Lab in a Second Life post on March 14, 2008 but remained chairman of the board. In 2010, Rosedale once again took over as interim CEO, stepping down four months later.

(continued from page 71)

second-language learning, English, and Chemistry. In addition, many companies have launched marketing endeavors on Second Life or attempted to bring offline products inworld, especially if these products are entertainment-oriented. For example, sports events, concerts, and art exhibitions are now hosted regularly in the Second Life universe. There are even some companies that generate real-world revenue from inworld activities, such as Rivers Run Red and Electric Sheep.

Ultimately, the wide range of detailed activities and environments available in Second Life and the amount of time that both individuals and companies spend in Second Life can make it difficult to dismiss the virtual world as a mere "game." In today's climate, virtual worlds hold very real implications for social interactions and the opportunity to create new ways of learning, doing business, performing, and engaging in nearly any other activity online.

ETHICS AND BEHAVIOR IN VIRTUAL WORLDS

Many who do not take part in virtual worlds are surprised to learn that virtual worlds raise ethical questions. After all, since virtual worlds are, by definition, not real worlds, it is reasonable to wonder whether any actions taken within a virtual world could be considered unethical. Indeed, it might seem strange to apply the labels "ethical" or "unethical" to actions taken within a virtual world. This is particularly true given the roots of virtual worlds in video games. Since the purpose of many video games is to kill, deceive, steal from, or otherwise harm other characters within the game, whether such characters are computer-controlled or human controlled, few would consider killing a video game character to be unethical if the rules of the game reward such killing. Even those who criticize the violence in video games typically do so because of the games' alleged tendency to spark violence in the real world, not for the reason that violence within the game is unethical.

Yet, as the preceding discussion illustrates, many virtual worlds today do not take the form of video games and do not have rules requiring or encouraging violence, theft, fraud, or other activities within the virtual world that would be considered unethical if performed in the real world. Furthermore, such virtual worlds often are inhabited by avatars controlled by real people in the real world. The people who control such avatars interact in the virtual world as they please. Virtual worlds provide users with an increasingly wide range of actions from which to choose.

As a result, the ethical line between actions in the real world and actions in the virtual world has begun to blur. For example, people may engage in conversations in a virtual world through their avatars. Such a conversation differs little from a conversation using a telephone or any other technology. Few would disagree that someone who directs racial epithets or other hurtful insults at someone else over the telephone acts unethically. This seems to imply that the same action within a virtual world would, or at least could, be unethical.

The situation, however, is not so simple, because virtual worlds can differ from telephones. For example, virtual worlds often allow people to adopt avatars that bear little or no resemblance to their real-world selves. People can take on an avatar that not only differs from their real physical appearance but also differs from their real-world personality. Most people who participate in virtual worlds are aware of this. Keeping this in mind, someone may intentionally adopt a racist personality in a virtual world, perhaps for the purpose of satirizing racism by engaging in exaggerated racist behavior or to help others practice responding to racist behavior in the real world by responding to it in the virtual world, where it is safe to do so. As a result, whether shouting racial insults in a virtual world is unethical may depend both on the context in which such activity occurs and on the knowledge and consent of other participants in the virtual world to such behavior.

Similar considerations apply to a variety of other actions that would clearly be considered unethical in the real world, such as lying, slander, and fraud. To the extent that users of virtual worlds do not intend for their avatars to represent their real selves and to the extent that they maintain a separation between actions in the virtual world and those in the real world, these activities carry little or none of the sting that they would in the real world and therefore are not unethical. Furthermore, the ability of people to adopt multiple avatars in a single virtual world may further dissipate the potential harm of seemingly unethical actions taken against them. For example, if someone spreads a false rumor within a virtual world about one avatar, that avatar's controller can discontinue using that avatar and begin using a new one, thereby potentially neutralizing the impact of the slander. In the real world, people only respond in this way in extreme situations, such as by moving to a new state and adopting a new identity. In contrast, switching avatars in a virtual world can be relatively easy, quick, and inexpensive. Even if someone who is the victim of a falsehood in a virtual world chose to keep using the same avatar, the victim may simply not care about the negative impact on the avatar's reputation as long as that impact does not spill over to the real world.

More difficult ethical questions arise in connection with people who are more significantly and psychologically invested in their inworld personas and engage in virtual world activities to interact with other people sincerely and out of a desire to honestly connect with others. For example, a group of friends who attended the same high school but who are now spread out across the real world might meet each other regularly within a virtual world. Such interactions may take on much the same flavor as real-world interactions. As a result, rumors, insults, harassment, and other actions that would be hurtful in the real world may be no less painful when experienced in the virtual world. Furthermore, given the expectation among everyone in the group that the avatars they are communicating with are being controlled by the people they resemble in the real world, someone who logs in as another member of the group to take control of that person's avatar and who then interacts with other group members under false pretenses may thereby engage in a serious breach of trust.

More generally, however, the question whether it is unethical to impersonate someone in a virtual world is complicated because the very nature of a virtual world requires each user to adopt an avatar that at most imperfectly resembles one's real self and may not resemble one's real self at all. Furthermore, many people within a virtual world may adopt avatars that appear identical or very

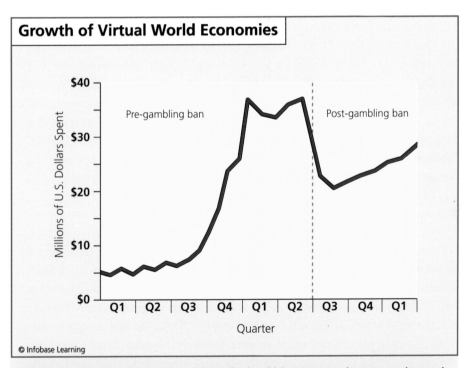

Growth of Virtual World Economies

Pre-gambling ban

Post-gambling ban

Millions of U.S. Dollars Spent

$40

$30

$20

$10

$0

Q1 Q2 Q3 Q4 Q1 Q2 Q3 Q4 Q1

Quarter

© Infobase Learning

Many virtual worlds have their own economies in which money can be spent and earned. As virtual worlds have grown increasingly popular, their virtual economies have grown correspondingly. As this graph shows, although the exponential growth of virtual economies was temporarily reversed when Second Life banned gambling (indicated by the red vertical line), the economies have begun to grow again since the ban took effect.

```
0011010100101001110101101010101011001010001
```

Virtual Rape: The LambdaMOO Case

An interesting and disturbing example of ethical dilemmas in virtual environments occurred in 1993 with the case of Lambda*MOO,* a text-based virtual community that at the time included thousands of members. Widely studied and discussed, this community experienced a "virtual rape" that led to a serious discussion of virtual ethics and the limits of online behavior. After witnessing the unfolding of this saga, writer Julian Dibbell published a widely reprinted piece entitled "A Rape in Cyberspace," which dissected the details of the incident.

Though significantly less popular today, LambdaMOO still exists as an online gathering space. Although the environment is meant to simulate a mansion, the interface includes no graphics or images. Instead, all actions and characters are described using text. Still, each user has sole control of his or her character and the descriptions that these characters produce.

One evening in 1993, a LambdaMOO user named Mr. Bungle used a "voodoo doll" program to impersonate various users, "forcing" them to perform sex acts on his character, each other, and themselves. Many of the so-called "victims" reported experiencing intense emotions as a result of this virtual harassment. Following the incident, the entire LambdaMOO community engaged in a lengthy discussion over whether any punishment would be leveled against Mr. Bungle. Eventually, his account was deleted by an administrator, but the debate over Mr. Bungle's actions raised a number of enduring questions about ethics online.

To begin with, there was the question whether this "virtual rape" was in fact unacceptable within the community. After all, there were no specific regulations against such behavior. No physical harm was caused. However, many users felt extreme anger toward Mr. Bungle for violating what they saw as basic ethical norms within the community. One victim noted that she had "post-traumatic tears streaming down her face." Following some notion of shared ethics, users then considered whether to punish Mr. Bungle. No community members made attempts to force legal action in the real world. However, intense debate emerged over whether virtual punishment could be meted out. Some users felt that Bungle's account should be terminated immediately, while others didn't feel comfortable with this kind of harsh pursuit of justice in the cyberspace arena. Eventually, the issue led to a complete restructuring of the LambdaMOO community.

```
0011010100101001110101101010101011001010001
```

similar. Some people may even intentionally and consensually share a single avatar. Therefore, it is difficult to draw a line between ethical adoption of a fictitious avatar and unethical adoption of someone else's avatar.

Furthermore, to the extent that inworld property increasingly is purchased with and otherwise tied to real-world money, theft of property within virtual worlds can be just as unethical as real-world theft. Even if inworld property is purchased with virtual money that has no connection to real-world money, the theft of such property could be considered unethical if the theft victim had engaged in significant effort to earn or otherwise obtain such property. If, however, inworld property can be created or otherwise obtained automatically or without any effort, it is less clear whether inworld theft constitutes unethical behavior.

Many of the ethical questions raised by virtual worlds result from the fact that insufficient time has passed for people to develop clear, shared expectations about what is permissible and impermissible within virtual worlds. As a result, different people come to virtual worlds with different expectations, many of which are reasonable but inconsistent. Although one way to solve this problem would be for companies, such as Linden Lab, that host virtual worlds to create and even impose rules on the inhabitants, strict regulation would strip virtual worlds of one of their most attractive features—the ability for participants to create new environments that differ from reality without externally imposed rules. Therefore, although it may be useful for some rules to be imposed to guard against the most egregious kinds of inworld behavior, the most prudent course may be to continue to allow inhabitants of virtual worlds to gradually work out the rules of engagement collectively, as people throughout the world have done in their own communities, cultures, and countries throughout history.

SHOULD VIRTUAL CRIMINALS FACE REAL-LIFE CONSEQUENCES?

Ethical violations within virtual worlds often do not result in any punishment within the virtual world or the real world. Some virtual worlds, however, have instituted rules and procedures for punishing ethical violations and the equivalent of unlawful actions within virtual worlds. For example, participants who repeatedly attempt to communicate with other characters who indicate their unwillingness to engage in conversation may be reprimanded or denied the right to chat with other participants for some period of time. Extreme or repeated violations may result in banishing the offending participant from the virtual world entirely. Decisions about punishment may be made by the company or other entity that hosts the virtual world or by a virtual jury consisting of other virtual world participants. Those who are convicted may even have their avatars displayed beyond bars within a virtual prison. Based on anecdotal evidence, such virtual punishments can be effective at deterring people from further misconduct because of the embarrassment and loss of virtual world privileges they encounter.

Some virtual worlds and real world courts have taken punishment a step further, prosecuting and convicting virtual world participants for real world crimes based on their virtual world activities. For example, a court in the Netherlands sentenced two youths to community service for stealing an inworld amulet and mask from another boy. Although the case involved real world threats—the perpetrators physically threatened the victim in his room with a knife—the court's ruling that the taking of inworld property constituted real world theft was based on the court's finding that *virtual property* was property under Dutch law.

As another example, in South Korea, virtual mafia and gangs have emerged within gaming environments, creating online crime rings to extort money from players in exchange for "protection." The South Korean government has already created a special police division to deal with these crimes, logging 22,000 cases in the first six months of operation. A woman in Japan was arrested on suspicion of illegally accessing a computer after she broke into her virtual husband's account on the interactive game MapleStory and killing his avatar there.

In addition, "cyberbrothels" have appeared within virtual worlds such as Second Life, in which users charge money (or virtual money) for minutes of cybersex. At times, these "institutions" have involved minors, giving authorities cause for alarm. "Virtual mugging" has also emerged, in which users create programs to steal and resell the property of others in online communities.

Still, the jury is out on whether these crimes can truly be targeted by real-world authorities, especially within the United States. Although scholars have discussed the issue in law journals, such as the *New York Law School Law Review* and the *California Criminal Law Review,* no definitive conclusions have emerged about whether activities performed solely online, without any corresponding physical harm or intimidation in the real world, can constitute real world crimes.

GRIEFERS: THE CYBERBULLIES OF VIRTUAL WORLDS

The term *griefing* originated in the late 1990s, when it was used to describe anti-social behavior that occurred in massively multiplayer games. *Griefers* are players who practice griefing by using hacking software or by exploiting glitches in the mechanics of a game to ruin the online experience for as many players as possible. Griefers represent the progression of virtual bullying that first appeared in early online communities such as LambdaMoo.

In the past decade, griefing has become an organized activity practiced by a growing subculture of people. Organized griefers take pleasure in causing frustration for people who are seriously involved in gaming, role-playing, and virtual worlds. Griefing can take many forms, from destroying other people's creations in a virtual world such as Second Life to ganging up together to disrupt a multiplayer game. In games and virtual worlds where the environment can be modified, griefers develop pranks and leave graffiti. They may steal from other players, stalk novice players, or conspire to get a player killed.

Game administrators often take swift action when griefers are detected, removing their accounts and banning them from the game or virtual environment. For subscription games and environments, griefers can hurt the bottom line. According to CNET News, griefer-related problems on some Web sites account for more than 25 percent of customer service calls. The dysfunctional behavior exhibited by griefers can force some players to abandon a game or virtual world. In virtual worlds with economies based on real-world money, griefer activities can cause players to lose real money.

Online games and virtual world Web sites have begun to fight griefers by encouraging their user communities to report harassment. Many games already have guild systems that allow like-minded players to group together. The next step in combating griefers may be the evolution of guild systems into virtual societies of players who develop their own laws and police their virtual environment.

CONCLUSIONS

Although virtual worlds are still in their infancy, they have already begun to raise a variety of ethical issues. Each time an ethical problem arises, it tends to be dismissed at first as trivial before becoming recognized as capable of causing real harm to real people. Even when people take on fictitious characters in virtual worlds, their feelings can still be hurt, just as people playing games in the real world can be offended, insulted, or embarrassed by others who consider themselves merely to be playing according to the rules of the game. The psychological harm inflicted on people participating in virtual worlds can be just as real as that inflicted through real world behavior because real people are involved.

Perhaps more surprisingly, even though assault, battery, kidnapping, and other violent crimes in virtual worlds cannot physically harm their victims, such virtual crimes can still create psychological harm. People who are victims of such crimes in the real world often report that it is more difficult to recover from the psychological effects of such crimes than the physical wounds. Therefore, perhaps it should not be so surprising that virtual crimes can have real effects on real people, especially when the victim had previously placed trust in the other inhabitants of the virtual world and had developed relationships with them involving real emotional bonds. Whether or not these actions are ever held to violate any laws in the real world, it is not difficult to see how breach of trust and intentional infliction of emotional pain can be unethical even when carried out through virtual actions. After all, despite the old adage that "sticks and stones may break my bones, but words shall never harm me," most people acknowledge that even though words cannot physically harm anyone, they can be just as psychologically painful as any physical attack. Therefore, anyone who takes part in a virtual world should think carefully about their actions there and not simply assume that virtual worlds are places where no ethical rules could ever apply.

5

PROFESSIONAL ETHICS: WHEN IS THE PROGRAMMER RESPONSIBLE?

Software bugs are errors that cause software to fail or behave in unexpected ways. The following is a list of examples of errors that are caused by bugs:

- prevent a Web browser from displaying videos stored in certain formats;
- cause a telephone company's billing software to calculate the wrong amount due on an invoice;
- lead a word processor to crash whenever an image is inserted into a document;
- allow an online bank account to be accessed even without providing the correct password; and
- cause the autopilot software on an airplane to miscalculate the airplane's altitude.

As these examples illustrate, bugs can vary widely in their causes and effects. They can range from mere annoyances that can be overlooked, to errors that cause financial harm, to dangerous flaws that could lead to physical injury or even death. Even when a software bug causes no measurable harm, it still causes the software's users to question the software's overall trustworthiness and reliability. In order to avoid this lack of trust and the more significant harms that software bugs can cause, one might think that software development organizations would strive to remove all known bugs from software before releasing that software to its customers.

In reality, however, bug-free software is a goal that is rarely attained. Instead, many software packages are released with known bugs that have been judged to be of the non-showstopper variety, meaning that the software vendor has decided that the bugs are not critical enough to delay release of the software.

The following are just a few of the reasons that software may be released with known bugs:

- Most software releases are calendar-driven, with release dates being announced by the software vendor to the public several months in advance. Customers make plans based on a promised software release date, and there is usually a competitive advantage to be gained by releasing software on schedule. Holding up a release to fix critical bugs is a serious business decision that can have a negative impact on a software company's reputation. Customers who were expecting the software to be released by a particular date may purchase a competitor's software if the software they were expecting is not released on time.

- Some bugs are very difficult to fix. Even when the symptoms of a bug are known, the bug's causes may be a mystery. For example, although a particular piece of software may crash roughly once per week, it may be very difficult to identify the particular circumstances that led to the crash. In this situation, the software vendor may decide to release the software to allow time for further testing and to obtain more detailed reports from the software's users of the circumstances surrounding crashes so that the vendor can use the information to isolate the causes of the bug.

- Some bugs are very expensive to fix. For example, a programmer may determine that a bug can only be fixed by rewriting a significant portion of the entire software package, an effort that may require several weeks or months of time. When faced with such a situation, a software company may decide that the problem is too expensive to fix immediately and decide to delay the fix until a future release.

- Many bug fixes bring with them the chance of regressions. This means that the act of fixing a bug may inadvertently introduce new bugs into the software. In cases in which the chance of regressions is great and there are limited testing resources available, a software vendor may decide that it is better to release software with a known, but minor, bug, rather than risk the chance of introducing an even more serious bug by fixing the known bug.

Even though it is common practice to release software with known bugs for the reasons listed above, doing so raises ethical and legal questions. Many software companies provide a list of *caveats* with each software release, describing the most serious bugs contained within the software. *Caveat* comes from the Latin phrase *caveat emptor,* "let the buyer beware." The implication is that the buyer of the software has been informed of the software's problems, that the buyer accepts the risk of using the software despite its flaws, and that the buyer implicitly agrees not to hold the seller responsible for problems that result from the flaws. In some cases, the software vendor may provide information about *workarounds,* which are steps that the buyer can take to avoid triggering the

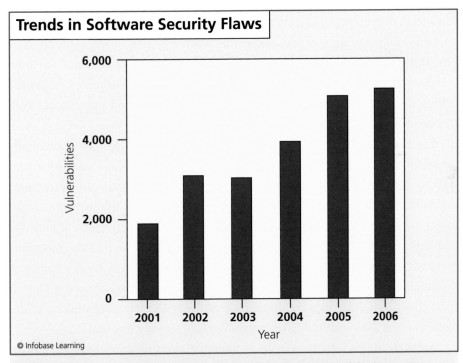

© Infobase Learning

Flaws in software security have been on the rise in the first decade of the 21st century despite the efforts of software giants such as Microsoft to keep such defects in check. (Statistics are only available through 2006.)

bug or to mitigate the consequences of the bug. For example, the vendor might inform users that they should change the resolution on their monitors if the software displays graphics using the wrong colors.

Software is one of the few products that customers have come to accept as having problems at the time of purchase. Most people would find it unacceptable if a new television came with a list of items that were not functioning correctly and would find the manufacturer ethically blameworthy for selling such a product, even if the seller provided documentation of the problems. Consumers of televisions and most other products expect the manufacturer to have worked out all flaws in the product before putting it on the market and even to remove features from the product that cannot be fixed.

Yet the commonly accepted standard of quality is lower for software than for most other products. Some argue that this is justified by the fact that computers and software are highly complex, more so than other products, and that this complexity makes it either impossible or prohibitively expensive for software vendors to deliver bug-free software. A single commercial software product may contain millions of lines of computer code written by tens or even hundreds of programmers. The size and complexity of such software and the need for large numbers of people to cooperate and communicate with each other to create such software increase the likelihood that bugs will be introduced into the software that are difficult or impossible to detect and fix.

For example, many computer programs involve some form of mathematical calculation, and bugs can occur due to mistakes in calculations. Math errors such as division by zero (which is mathematically undefined) can cause bugs, and such bugs may be difficult to detect unless and until the software is run under conditions in which division by zero occurs. In other words, it may not be possible to detect such a bug merely by reading the code that the programmers wrote. Instead, it may be necessary to consider the very large number of situations that the software might encounter and to test the software under all such conditions. This may be difficult or prohibitively time-consuming to do, particularly if the conditions that trigger the bug are very unusual.

Software stores data in computer memory. Each memory location has an address that is used to access the memory location. For example, software might store the number 12 in a memory location having address number 300. To retrieve the number 12 later, the software must refer to memory address number

300. If the software calculates the memory address incorrectly, this may cause the wrong data to be retrieved or even cause the computer to crash if the memory address is invalid (such as a negative memory address).

Typographical errors ("typos") in software's source code can also cause bugs. For example, programmers use variables in source code to store data. Each variable has a name. As a simple example, imagine that a programmer is writing source code to find the average of two numbers and has created two variables named "number1" and "number2." The source code must define values for number1 and number2, then add them together and divide the sum by 2. In the course of writing the source code, the programmer may mistakenly type "number1 + number1" instead of "number1 + number2." This typing mistake will

---

Minor Typographical Error Creates a Major Bug

```
void bubbleSort (int *array, int length)
{
   int i, j, temp;
   int test; /*use this only if unsure whether the list is already
sorted or not*/
   for (i = length - 1; i > 0; i - -)
   {
    test=0;
    for(j = 0; j < i; j++)
    {
     if (array[j] > array[j+1]) /* compare neighboring elements */
     {
       temp = array[j];   /* swap array[j] and array[j+1] */
       array[j] = array[j+1];
       array[j+1] = temp;
       test=1;
     }
    } /*end for j*/
    if (test = = 0) break; /*will exit if the list is sorted!*/
   } /*end for i*/

} /*end bubbleSort*/
```

```
void bubbleSort (int *array, int length)
{
   int i, j, temp;
   int test; /*use this only if unsure whether the list is already
sorted or not*/
   for (i = length - 1; i > 0; i - -)
   {
    test=0;
    for(j = 0; j < i; j++)
    {
     if (array[j] > array[j+1]) /* compare neighboring elements */
     {
       temp = array[j];   /* swap array[j] and array[j+1] */
       array[j] = array[j+1];
       array[j+1] = temp;
       test=1;
     }
    } /*end for j*/
    if (test = 0) break; /*will exit if the list is sorted!*/
   } /*end for i*/

} /*end bubbleSort*/
```

© Infobase Learning

Computer programmers create software by writing source code. Even seemingly minor typographical errors in source code can create significant bugs in the resulting software. This example shows two sets of source code that are identical except for the highlighted difference. The version on the left-hand side correctly uses the double equals sign in the C programming language to determine whether the value of the variable named test is equal to zero. The version on the right-hand side represents a typographical error, which uses the single equals sign to assign the value of zero to the variable named test. This single-character error will cause the software to behave differently than intended. Such an error can be very difficult to detect either manually or automatically.

cause the software to calculate the wrong value when the software runs. Even very minor typographical errors can result in significant bugs and be very difficult to detect and fix. For example, it is easy to mistakenly type the capital letter O instead of the number 0 or the lowercase letter l instead of the number 1, yet such typos are very difficult to find.

The categories of bugs just described involve errors introduced into the source code by programmers. Other kinds of bugs result from miscommunication among different people working on a software development project. Consider a software company that has planned certain functionality in its next software release, such as the ability to check the spelling of a document. The task of coding this functionality is given to a developer, but the requirements are not clearly specified, leading the developer to believe that his job is to create a grammar checker rather than a spelling checker. The developer then writes code for a grammar checker. Although the developer's code may perform the task that he intended it to perform perfectly, it might still be considered a bug if it does not do what the software's architect wanted it to do. If the difference between what was intended and what was created is minor, such bugs can be difficult to detect, just as two people can engage in a conversation about slightly different topics for some period of time before realizing that they are not talking about the same thing.

Another category of bugs relates to complex software systems that perform several calculations at once. For example, e-mail software might include one component for displaying e-mail messages on the screen and another component for downloading new e-mail into the user's inbox. Both components may execute in parallel (at the same time as each other). Bugs may occur in such systems due to unforeseen ways in which the timing of components interacts. For example, a *deadlock* bug involves two or more software components that are each waiting for the others to complete, with the result that none of the processes can complete. This type of bug can be difficult to diagnose and fix since the exact conditions that caused the bug must be replicated but may only occur in unusual circumstances.

Although bugs may be caused by something as trivial as a typing error, the impact of a software bug can vary from inconsequential to disastrous. Among video gamers, bugs are referred to as glitches and are sometimes used to a player's advantage, such as by walking through walls that were intended by the programmer to be solid. Most glitches are not viewed in a negative light unless they

The voyage of the *Mariner 1* space probe, shown here lifting off from Cape Kennedy Launch Complex 12 in 1962, was destructively aborted due to a software bug in the probe's guidance system that would otherwise have led the probe to crash, possibly in an inhabited area. Although the precise nature of the bug remains in dispute, according to some accounts the error consisted of a single missing mathematical symbol. *(NASA)*

have a serious impact on the gaming experience. As another example of a non-serious software bug, consider a word processing application such as Microsoft Word that has a spellchecker. Suppose there are a few spelling errors that the spellchecker cannot detect. A user of Word may never encounter this problem, and even if the problem does occur, at worst it will lead to a misspelled word becoming part of the final document.

Many real disasters, however, have occurred because of software bugs. An American computer scientist named Peter G. Neumann maintains a list of catastrophic failures caused by software bugs and has written a number of articles and a book entitled *Computer-Related Risks* on the subject. The most serious disasters involve nuclear power, which has the potential to cause large numbers of casualties. According to Neumann, the Three Mile Island nuclear power plant accident in 1979, the worst nuclear accident in U.S. history, was caused by a combination of human misjudgments, equipment failures, and software bugs. Sensors capable of detecting very high temperatures had been installed, but the software that read the sensor data suppressed readings that were outside a predefined range. For temperatures above 700 degrees, a series of question marks were printed in place of the actual temperature, masking the danger of a meltdown as temperatures approached 4,000 degrees. Although the nuclear power industry claims there were no human casualties as a result of the accident, estimates of the financial costs are at about $1 billion.

Another often-cited example of a catastrophic software failure involved a Canadian medical device known as the Therac-25 radiation therapy machine. A type of bug known as a race condition could, under certain circumstances, cause the machine to deliver a lethal dose of radiation. In 1985, three people died and another three were critically injured because of this bug. Since the bug only occurred under very specific startup conditions, it took some time to diagnose the software problem, resulting in unnecessary accidental deaths.

Software bugs can be harmful from both the perspective of human safety and business. Many software companies have recognized their ethical and legal responsibilities to eliminate software bugs and have put processes in place to find bugs before software is released and to evaluate known bugs for their severity. Some organizations have developed tools to help software programmers spot bugs before they occur. For example, after writing a piece of code, a programmer can use a tool to check for common syntax errors and poor programming style. Another methodology that has been adopted is to have programmers inspect each other's code, with the goal of finding errors that can lead to bugs. Finally, most software organizations have adopted rigorous procedures for testing software before releasing it. This can involve both human and automated testing. Human testing requires test engineers or software developers to repeatedly execute the software under various conditions and to look for situations in which bugs occur. Automated testing uses additional software that has been written to automatically run the software and look for problems in computations.

IMPACT OF PERSONAL VALUES OF THE PROGRAMMER

As shown in the previous section's discussion about software bugs, programmers play a pivotal role in the quality of software. Despite processes that many software organizations have put into place to reduce software bugs, the skills, attitudes, and values of individual software programmers can have a major impact on the quality of the software product. Programmers who feel disconnected from their work or unhappy with their employer are less likely to put in the extra effort to produce high-quality code.

Another way that a programmer's values can have an impact on software is when system requirements are not completely defined and decisions are left up to the programmer. For example, consider a programmer who believes that it is the responsibility of the software's users to figure out how the software works. When such a programmer is instructed to program painting software that contains a particular set of features, such as the ability to draw lines, squares, and circles, the programmer might make the commands for performing these functions complicated and difficult to discover. He might also not include any online help within the software. The result is that although the programmer has followed the instructions he was given to create painting software that allows users to draw pictures, he has done so in a way that was influenced by his personal values, according to which software does not need to be easy to use. Different programmers with different values who are given the same programming assignment might all create very different software, because the end result could be influenced by the particular programmer's values in each case.

The effects of programmers' values often are felt when a school, business, or government agency attempts to modernize its operations by transferring existing information and processes from paper files to computers. For example, many courts have begun to require parties in lawsuits to submit their legal briefs and other documents in electronic form. The courts often purchase special software and hire programmers to create software for storing, editing, viewing, and managing such documents. If the software does not include sufficient tools to enable judges to write notes on the electronic documents they receive, then the judges may need to print the documents in order to write on them, thereby defeating the purpose of the electronic system, or stop taking notes. This is one example of a way in which attempts to "merely" take existing operations and move them online can actually cause such operations to change, even when no change was intended, as a result of programmers implicitly importing their own values into the software they create.

The previous examples generally illustrate ways in which programmers' values can unintentionally influence the software they create. More perniciously, a dishonest and malicious programmer may intentionally and secretly insert harmful code into software. For example, a programmer may insert a *back door* into a company's accounting software that allows the programmer to later access confidential financial data that the company believes can only be accessed by authorized accountants in possession of a secure password. Because software can be so complex and difficult to understand, it may be hard even for the company that employs the programmer to know that the programmer has inserted such a back door into the software. This is one reason why software that performs critical functions for banks, utility companies, and the military often is subject to extensive *code review* by third parties, which involves hiring professional programmers to scour the program's source code for bugs, whether intentional or unintentional, before the program is put into use in real world conditions.

It is not always undesirable for programmers' values to influence the software they create. A programmer with an artistic flair who creates a Web browser with an attractive user interface may make using the software more satisfying. The difference between this example and the others described above is that in the case of the artistic Web browser, the programmer's influence is immediately apparent to anyone who uses the software. In contrast, when software lacks features or contains bugs or Trojan horses as a result of the programmer's values, the programmer's influence will likely remain hidden from the end user, and as a result the end user may not have a choice about whether to accept or reject the programmer's values and the consequences of such values. Therefore, it will

(continues on page 94)

`100111010010101010011001011101101010010101001`

Ramon C. Barquin and the Ten Commandments of Computer Ethics

The Computer Ethics Institute (CEI) originated in 1985 as the Coalition for Computer Ethics. Founders of the organization included employees of IBM and members of the Brookings Institution, a Washington, D.C., nonprofit think tank. At the time CEI was formed, little was being done to define ethical standards for information technology. CEI was one of the first organizations to focus on public policy and ethical issues related to advances in computing. CEI served as a forum for discussion among corporate, academic, and government sectors about the moral implications of technology and the need for regulation, legislation, and the creation of best practices.

In 1992, a set of standards called the Ten Commandments of Computer Ethics was introduced in a CEI-sponsored paper by Dr. Ramon C. Barquin. The purpose of the commandments was to define a set of guidelines for the ethical use of computers. Barquin borrowed from the style of the Bible's Ten Commandments, including use of archaic wording such as "thou shalt not." The following is a list of Barquin's Ten Commandments (which can be found on the CEI Web site at http://www.computerethicsinstitute.com/publications/tencommandments.html):

1. Thou shalt not use a computer to harm other people.
2. Thou shalt not interfere with other people's computer work.
3. Thou shalt not snoop around in other people's files.
4. Thou shalt not use a computer to steal.
5. Thou shalt not use a computer to bear false witness.
6. Thou shalt not use or copy software for which you have not paid.
7. Thou shalt not use other people's computer resources without authorization.
8. Thou shalt not appropriate other people's intellectual output.
9. Thou shalt think about the social consequences of the program you write.
10. Thou shalt use a computer in ways that show consideration and respect.

These commandments represent a good effort at identifying the ethical issues related to computers, but like most standards they are very general and lacking in

(continues)

`100111010010101010011001011101101010010101001`

001101010010100111010110101010101011001010000

(continued)

details that would provide more guidance for specific circumstances. For example, number 2, Thou shalt not interfere with other people's computer work, is open to wide interpretation. Surely, it does not include children and other family members who are spending too much time online or people who are using computers for illegal or harmful activities (such as identity theft). On the other hand, the concise form of these commandments makes them easy to understand and easy to remember.

As a result, these commandments can be taken as a good starting point for thinking about ethical behavior when using technology. As simplistic as the commandments may seem, they reflect many of the most pressing problems related to misuse of computers. This is somewhat remarkable, considering that when the commandments were devised in 1992 the World Wide Web had only just been invented and was not in widespread use. Yet the commandments seem to anticipate hackers, malware, and identity theft. Number 5, Thou shalt not use a computer to bear false witness, covers people who misrepresent themselves on social media sites such as Facebook and in virtual worlds such as Second Life. Number 8, Thou shalt not appropriate other people's intellectual output, pertains to the opportunities for students, researchers, and writers to easily plagiarize content from the Internet.

Dr. Ramon C. Barquin, whose background is in electrical engineering and mathematics, is a former IBM executive who has taught at MIT, the Chinese University of Hong Kong, and the University of Maryland. Dr. Barquin currently leads the Computer Ethics Institute and is the CEO of a private consulting firm, Barquin International, that specializes in data management and storage. He continues to publish articles on the technical and management aspects of information technology.

001101010010100111010110101010101011001010000

(continued from page 92)

likely always be necessary to take a variety of steps to protect users from such hidden values embedded in software, such as instructing programmers in computer ethics, requiring programmers to make legally enforceable agreements not to intentionally insert harmful bugs into software, and performing thorough code reviews of any software that could cause significant harm to the public.

`10011101001010101001100101110110101001010 01`

Terry Bynum (Southern Connecticut State University Professor of Philosophy, Computer Ethics Expert)

Terrell (Terry) Ward Bynum was born in 1938. He received bachelor's degrees in chemistry and philosophy from the University of Delaware, a master's degree in philosophy from Princeton, and both a M. Phil. and a Ph.D. in philosophy from the City University of New York. He has been a Fulbright Scholar, studying at the University of Bristol in England, a Danford and Woodrow Wilson Fellow at Princeton, a Mellon Fellow at the City University of New York, and a Dartmouth Fellow at Dartmouth College.

Professor Bynum's interests lie in the areas of computing and human values, topics on which he has published numerous books and articles. In 1968, he created the scholarly publication *Metaphilosophy*, which he edited for 25 years. He has also written on the topics of history of philosophy, education, logic and psychology and developed the Web site for the Research Center on Computing and Society into an influential research and teaching resource for computer ethics issues. The Web site contains a variety of articles, monographs, and compilations on various subtopics within the field of computer ethics. In 1991, together with Walter Maner of Bowling Green State University in Ohio, Bynum created the National Conference on Computing and Values, hosted by Southern Connecticut State University and funded by the National Science Foundation. The purpose of the conference was to

Southern Connecticut State University professor Terrell (Terry) Warn Bynum, computer ethics expert *(Isabel Chenoweth, SCSU)*

(continues)

`100111010010101010100110010111011010100101 001`

0011010100101001110101101010101011001010100001

(continued)

attract computer professionals, philosophers, business leaders, and other influential thinkers who could work with the Research Center on Computing and Society after the conference. Four hundred people from all over the United States and seven foreign countries attended the conference, which generated a large number of publications and teaching resources.

Four years later in 1995, while a visiting professor at De Montfort University, Bynum teamed up with De Montfort professor Simon Rogerson to create a Centre for Computing and Social Responsibility as well as the first computer ethics conference in Europe, ETHICOMP95, which took place in Leicester. Walter Maner delivered the keynote address at the conference. ETHICOMP became a series of computer ethics conferences that took place every 18 months after ETHICOMP95; it was held in Spain, the Netherlands, Italy, Poland, Portugal, Greece, Sweden, and Japan. In 1999, Bynum and Rogerson assisted John Weckert and Christopher Simpson in creation of the Australian Institute of Computer Ethics, as well as the AICE99 conference, which was the first international computer ethics conference not held in the Northern Hemisphere.

In 2004, Professor Bynum presented a concept paper entitled "Leapfrogging the Grid" at the World Energy Technologies Summit held at the UNESCO headquarters in Paris, France. The paper explored the idea of using of miniaturized electronic devices, such as microcomputer circuits, to help a poor undeveloped village "leapfrog" into the information age without first going through the industrial age. The paper described various technologies that could make such a task possible.

Professor Bynum is currently a professor of philosophy at Southern Connecticut State University, where he is also a director of the Research Center on Computing and Society that he created in 1987. Professor Bynum is also a visiting professor at De Montfort University in Leicester, England.

0011010100101001110101101010101011001010100001

WHO IS RESPONSIBLE FOR SOFTWARE FLAWS?

When software causes harm, it is worth considering who is responsible for that harm—the programmer(s) who created the software, the company that employed the programmer, or perhaps even the end user who ran the software. Intuitively, one could understand how any of the three might be responsible.

Certainly the programmers, who wrote the code for the software, might be ethically responsible if they knew or should have known that the software would be harmful. Similarly, the company might have an ethical duty to review its software for potentially harmful bugs before releasing it to the public. Even the user might be responsible for using otherwise harmless software in a harmful way, such as when the user uses painting software to modify a photograph to make it appear as if someone was present in a jewelry store during a robbery in order to influence the police to make a false arrest.

Although one might be tempted to turn to the law for guidance on which of these three parties should be held liable, the law has had difficulty drawing such conclusions, in part because software appears to fall into multiple categories simultaneously. For example, under principles of tort law and the First Amendment to the U.S. Constitution, someone who writes and publishes instructions for performing a crime usually is not legally responsible for someone else who reads the instructions and engages in the crime. Only the person who actually commits the crime violates the law. On one hand, source code for a program that can shut down a power plant is a set of instructions. This would lead to the conclusion that someone who writes and publishes such source code should not be legally responsible for someone else who uses the source code to create software and then runs that software to shut down a power plant. On the other hand, however, because the source code can be converted into functioning software so quickly, easily, and automatically, distributing such source code appears similar to conspiring with other people to use the software to shut down power plants. The ease of converting from source code instructions to running software, in other words, blurs the line between the two. Therefore, the law does not provide very clear guidance about whether the programmer is responsible for shutting down the power plant.

The same problem makes it difficult to draw a conclusion about who is ethically responsible. In the example given above, it seems clear that the end user who intentionally uses software to shut down a power plant is ethically responsible for causing people to lose power. However, this does not mean that end users are always ethically responsible for harm caused by the software they run. For example, in many situations the end user might not even be aware that software on his or her computer is doing anything harmful. If someone's computer is infected by a virus, that virus might be triggered secretly and automatically every time the user sends an e-mail message. Yet it would seem unfair to consider the user ethically responsible for spreading the virus every time he or she sends an e-mail message, because even though the e-mail message was sent intentionally, the virus was not spread intentionally. This conclusion might change, however, if the user recklessly ignored signs that the virus was running, such as by ignoring warning messages displayed by the computer's antivirus software.

Because of the difficulty of assigning responsibility to either the programmer or the end user, it might seem tempting to conclude that the buck should stop with the company, government agency, or other organization that releases the software to the public. Certainly, one of the roles played by such an entity is to ensure that software it releases meets minimum standards for quality and security. From a legal perspective, responsibility would almost always fall with the company rather than its programmers. The ethical question, however, is not as simple. Even the most diligent company cannot police every line of code written by every employee. A disgruntled employee might intentionally deceive the company into believing that software was bug-free when in fact it contained a virus. Although it might make sense to hold the company legally responsible for practical reasons, if the company had taken every reasonable step to prevent bugs from entering its software the company's hands might be clean from an ethical perspective.

One way to mesh the practical and the ethical is to adopt practices used widely in other professions, such as medicine and law, that require formal testing, certification, and licensing before individuals are allowed to practice within the profession. For example, a professional structural engineer must become licensed in order to be allowed to sign off on engineering drawings that will be used in construction of homes, offices, and other buildings. The engineer can be held personally liable for errors that are subsequently found in the drawings. Computer programmers are not typically required to obtain such certification before they can create software professionally. Although most major software companies prefer programmers to have at least an undergraduate degree in computer science or a related field, many professional programmers are self-taught or have a degree in an unrelated field.

Instead of professional licensing of software developers, the Association for Computing Machinery (ACM), the leading industry association for computer professionals, has formulated a Code of Ethics and Professional Conduct that attempts to address most ethical issues encountered by professional programmers. The Code consists of general imperatives such as "Contribute to society and human well-being" and "Avoid harm to others." In addition to the Code, the ACM has published a set of guidelines that provide more details about specific applications of the Code.

In 2009, the European Union (EU) Commission proposed an expansion of its consumer protection policy to include guarantees for the quality of software products. The EU Sales and Guarantees Directive requires that firms offer two-year guarantees on tangible consumer goods. Licensed software has been exempt from the directive, but EU commissioners would like to see a change to require retailers to provide a refund for a video game or other software product that has a bug or glitch that makes it unusable. Some software developers oppose the directive, arguing that software is not a tangible good. Once again, this illustrates how the difficulty of fitting software within preexisting categories can make assigning responsibility for the quality, security, and safety of software particularly difficult.

CONCLUSIONS

Determining who is ethically responsible for software bugs is not as simple as it first seems. One cannot pin responsibility on the programmer in all cases, nor on the software vendor or the software's user. In some sense, this is no different from the case of other products, such as automobiles, in which responsibility might lie with the automotive engineer, automobile manufacturer, or individual driver in different situations depending on the circumstances. The situation with software, however, is more complex, not only because individual pieces of software can be highly complex, but because so many different pieces of software can run on the same computer and interact with other software over the Internet. As a result, many people are involved not only in the creation but also in the use of any particular piece of software. This makes it difficult to clearly identify the role of each person and that person's corresponding responsibility for any harm caused by software running on a computer.

Furthermore, computers are designed to be updated with new software. Computer users frequently buy, download, and install new Web browsers, video games, and finance software onto their computers. Businesses routinely update the antivirus software on their computers and upgrade to the latest version of their industry's billing software. Computers even automatically update themselves by downloading and installing patches to their operating systems overnight. This further complicates the relationships among the many people who are responsible for the software running on any particular computer. For example, the instant messaging software that a user installs on her computer may not even have existed when the computer was first designed. This raises the question whether the computer's manufacturer could ever be considered ethically responsible for harm caused by that instant messaging software. Yet everyone knows that computers are designed to be updated frequently, so perhaps computer manufacturers need to take this into account by designing computer hardware that is resilient in the face of new software.

Computer ethics, therefore, can be even more complicated than the ethics related to the design, sale, and use of traditional technology. The very flexibility that makes computers universal machines and the very interconnectedness that makes the Internet so valuable also create a complex web of connections among software and people that will likely require much additional thought and debate before any degree of agreement is reached about the ethical responsibilities of those who create software.

6

COPYING: DOES EASE OF COPYING MAKE IT RIGHT?

Today's widespread use of computers and the Internet for research has facilitated copying the work of others and therefore increased the temptation to do so. It is relatively easy to use widely available software, such as Web browsers and word processors, combined with the universal copy and paste function, to repurpose text and photographs from other works and pass them off as one's own. However, the ease of copying from the work of others on the Internet does not lessen the ethical implications of such copying. If anything, the ease, speed, and low cost of copying may raise the ethical stakes.

According to the *Merriam-Webster Dictionary,* to plagiarize is "to steal and pass off (the ideas or words of another) as one's own" and "to use (another's production) without crediting the source." The problem of *plagiarism* has been around for hundreds of years, with the word "plagiarism" first appearing in the *Oxford English Dictionary* in 1621, five years after the death of playwright and poet William Shakespeare. Indeed, Shakespeare is generally acknowledged to have borrowed some of his plots from the works of earlier writers.

There are different degrees of plagiarism. The most clear-cut kind of plagiarism is that in which someone copies another's work verbatim and claims it as one's own original work. This is an act of fraud similar to counterfeiting. Schools universally prohibit their students and teachers from engaging in plagiarism. Several cases of outright plagiarism by prominent authors, journalists, and music composers have received media attention in the past few years. Besides being the focus of media coverage, some cases of plagiarism even make their way to the legal system, with the author whose work was plagiarized taking action against the copier for copyright *infringement* and other legally actionable offenses. These cases illustrate both that plagiarism is widely accepted as an act harmful to the author whose work was plagiarized and can have serious consequences for the plagiarist.

With the instant availability of breaking news stories on the Internet, it has become easier for journalists to engage in plagiarism. Plagiarism is a serious accusation against a professional journalist, since it undermines the reliability of both the journalist and the journalist's employer. When a journalist working for a major newspaper is discovered to have plagiarized a story, it usually becomes national news. One such case involving a young reporter working for the *New York Times* is included here to illustrate the serious ethical issues that are at the heart of plagiarism.

Jayson Blair was a 26-year-old reporter who, between 1999 and 2003, worked his way up from an intern to prestigious national reporting assignments, despite having been criticized for the number of mistakes and inaccuracies in his stories. He was assigned to cover important news, such as the Beltway sniper attacks (a series of murders in the Washington D.C. area) and the war in Iraq, but continued to be faulted for reporting errors. At one point, a prosecutor held a news conference to denounce Blair's coverage of the Beltway sniper case.

Blair had written more than 600 stories for the *New York Times* when he finally was exposed in April 2003 for plagiarizing a story from the *San Antonio Express-News*. Blair had copied details and quotes related to an interview with a San Antonio woman directly from the other story. Further investigation revealed that Blair had plagiarized in many of his articles, including taking credit for interviews that had been conducted by other reporters. It was subsequently discovered that he had not only plagiarized from the work of other journalists but had also fabricated information for his stories.

Jayson Blair resigned from his position and has not worked as a journalist since. The *New York Times* rushed to conduct an internal investigation to discover how a young reporter who had been suspected of questionable professional ethics could have advanced so quickly up the ranks without detection. The integrity of the paper was placed in serious doubt because of his actions and the lack of editorial control over his work.

The Jayson Blair case was clearly one of plagiarism. Other situations may not be as clear-cut. Books and essays often contain quotations from the works of other writers; this practice is widely considered to be ethical as long as the

Fernand Léger's 1930 painting *Mona Lisa with Keys* is an example of artwork that combines the work of others (namely, Leonardo da Vinci's Mona Lisa) with additional artistic elements. Controversy often arises over whether such use of other's artwork constitutes unethical copying or creative and ethical transformation of existing images into a new work of art.   *(Réunion des musées nationaux/Art Resource, NY; ©2010, Artists Rights Society (ARS), New York/ADAGP, Paris)*

original work is given attribution, usually in the form of a footnote pointing out the original source and its author. This is the most accepted way for an author to incorporate the work of others without engaging in plagiarism. Attribution gives proper credit to the original source and does not attempt to pass off the quoted work as the author's own. More subtle forms of using the work of others involve changing some of the words in a written work to make it appear original or using so many ideas from another source that it is in essence being copied. Even experts can disagree over whether such acts constitute plagiarism or merely sloppy writing.

In the world of academia, plagiarism by students or professors is a serious offense that can result in academic censure, a failing grade, suspension, or expulsion. In the past, students who were unwilling to spend time researching and writing an original work or felt pressured to receive a high grade might commit plagiarism by using the work of another student or by visiting the library and copying from a reference book or encyclopedia. Later, companies were created that would write papers for students for a fee, so that the students could pass off the commissioned works as their own. Today, the Internet has made it easier than ever to plagiarize, by providing access to such a wide variety of written works from which large portions of text and images can be copied with just a few keystrokes. Furthermore, companies that sell term papers now find it easier than ever to market their services to willing students over the Internet.

There was a time when students could freely copy from Internet sources with minimal fear of detection. Then Web sites, such as Turnitin.com, were developed to detect plagiarism in academic works. Teachers who subscribe to this type of Web site have their students submit papers in electronic form using the Web site's tools. Each paper is compared automatically to a very large database consisting of text from Web pages, student papers, academic journals, and books. Any plagiarized or improperly quoted passages are reported back to the teacher. Although the Internet has made plagiarism easier, Web sites such as Turnitin.com have now made it more difficult. They have not, however, made it impossible, and many students still copy from the Internet.

Some students who commit plagiarism may harbor a misunderstanding about the ethics of copying. Whether or not such plagiarism is unethical should not depend on how easy it is to detect. Activities such as buying a previously written research paper or paying someone else to write a new paper are clear cases of cheating, but many people consider information on the Internet to be in the *public domain* and freely available for copying. Others may be unaware that it may be permissible to copy entire sections of text from another source in some situations so long at the original source is clearly and correctly marked as a quotation and given appropriate attribution. The dividing line between permissible copying with attribution and plagiarism varies from circumstance to circumstance. As a result, many schools and educators have created guidelines to help students understand exactly what constitutes plagiarism in particular situations and how quoted text should be handled. Students who study the guidelines and try their best to follow them will not only avoid punishment in school, but will prepare themselves to enter the professional world, in which plagiarism is not only frowned upon but can lead to being fired from a job or even becoming the subject of a lawsuit.

INCORPORATING SOMEONE ELSE'S WORK INTO YOUR OWN

There are both laws and professional rules of ethics that govern the use of copyrighted material, and professional authors, musicians, and other artists must be aware of such rules as they create new works. Even students and nonprofessionals who may not be bound by legal rules regarding plagiarism must be aware of the ethics and consequences of plagiarism. As mentioned above, many educational institutes now provide resources to help students, teachers, and others avoid plagiarism, given how difficult it can be to make decisions about whether copying constitutes plagiarism in borderline cases. One such resource is the Purdue OWL (Online Writing Lab) Web site (http://owl.english.purdue.edu), which is maintained by the Purdue University Writing Lab. According to OWL, the best way to avoid plagiarism is to give credit where credit is due. In addition to giving guidance on *how* to give credit using the appropriate citation form (e.g., MLA or APA), OWL also educates students about *when* they should give credit. OWL suggests providing attribution for *any* words, ideas, or productions that an author uses that are not original to the author. This includes not only words from printed materials, songs, movies, and Web sites, but also words and ideas from interviews and face-to-face conversations, as well as copies of all types of visual and digital materials.

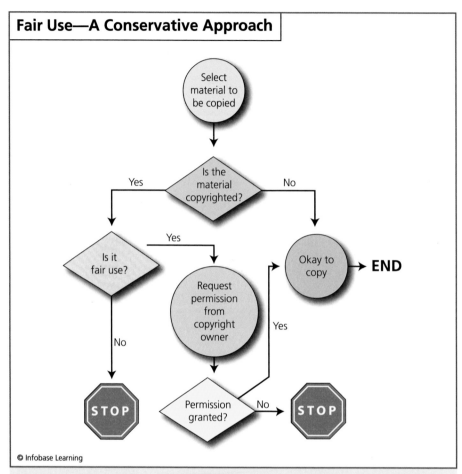

Fair Use—A Conservative Approach

Select material to be copied

Is the material copyrighted?
Yes / No

Is it fair use?
Yes

Request permission from copyright owner

Okay to copy → **END**

No

STOP

Permission granted?
No → STOP
Yes

© Infobase Learning

It can be difficult to determine whether copying existing copyrighted material constitutes permissible fair use under copyright law in a specific instance or whether such copying constitutes copyright infringement prohibited by the law. Although there are no hard and fast rules for making such determinations, this flow chart represents a process that can be used as a guideline for determining whether copying an existing copyrighted work is permissible or impermissible under copyright law.

Given this long list of content that needs to be attributed, it may at first seem unclear what does *not* need to be provided with attribution. However, a very wide variety of original words, images, music, and other content may be included in one's own work without attribution. Most obvious are one's own experiences, thoughts, creations, and conclusions. The OWL Web site also lists

(continues on page 108)

`1001110100101010100110010111011010100101001`

Shawn Fanning (Founder of Napster Online "File Sharing" Service)

Born in 1980 in Brockton, Massachusetts, Shawn Fanning became a household name at the age of 19 following the release of a file-sharing program he wrote in his freshman year at Northeastern University in Boston. This program, called Napster after Shawn's nickname, was able to transform individual computers into file-sharing servers for exchanging MP3 music files over the Internet.

Fanning grew up in Brockton and showed significant academic promise. In Shawn's sophomore year of high school, his uncle John gave him his first computer, an Apple Macintosh 512+, as well as an Internet connection and a separate phone line so that Shawn could surf the Internet. Shawn spent summers in high school as an intern working for his uncle's firm. Many interns at the company were Carnegie Mellon University graduates, and Shawn soon knew that he too wanted to go to Carnegie Mellon to study computer science. However, Carnegie Mellon rejected him and instead he went to Northeastern University. Even though Shawn was enrolled in advanced junior and senior courses, he was bored and disliked college.

What did catch Shawn's interest was his roommate's collection of MP3 music files. He started his own collection and quickly introduced the idea to

Shawn Fanning, the founder of the Napster Peer-to-Peer (P2P) file-sharing service, shown here at a press conference in San Francisco in 2001. Although the original incarnation of Napster was shut down after a court held that the service infringed copyrights, the service has since been transformed into a legitimate music-sharing service owned and operated by Best Buy. *(John G. Mabanglo/ AFP/Getty Images)*

(continues)

`1001110100101010100110010111011010100101001`

001101010010100111010110101010101011001010100001

(continued)

John. Worried about Shawn's lack of interest in academics, John let him take on a project of his own choosing: a music application that was able to track down MP3 files in a more efficient ways than other search engines available at the time. Suddenly, Shawn was working 16 hours a day, and his uncle could not have been happier with his nephew's newfound focus. He backed Shawn's decision to drop out of Northeastern to pursue the project full time. Together with Sean Parker and Jordan Ritter, Shawn worked tirelessly on finishing the *file-sharing software* that became Napster.

The first beta version of Napster was ready on June 1, 1999. Shawn gave the software to about 30 friends he met in online chat rooms for testing under the condition that they would not tell anyone about the project just yet. These initial beta testers did not heed Shawn's request for secrecy; in a few days, Napster had been downloaded more than 10,000 times. It continued to spread like wildfire, especially among the college-aged population. By 2000, more than 130 colleges had banned the program due to the strain it put on their networks.

The program worked by connecting users, about 2,000 to 5,000 per regular session, and allowing them to browse each other's computers for music files. Napster's success encouraged other peer-to-peer file-sharing programs, such as Gnutella, which operated on a similar principle of providing a medium over which people could share music files.

001101010010100111010110101010101011001010100001

(continued from page 106)

items of common knowledge, including folklore, myths, urban legends, generally known historical events, and generally accepted facts (such as "smoking is bad for your health").

Good students realize that citing sources gives their research more credibility. Using quotes from informed sources makes writing more interesting and in many cases can be used to make a point more effectively than completely original writing. However, it is possible to overuse quotations and end up with a written work that consists primarily of a series of quotations from other works strung together. Such work lacks originality and fails to demonstrate to the student's

Shawn's biggest contribution was not the creation of Napster, but that he forever changed the way in which people view music. Before Napster, if someone wanted to listen to a song, he or she needed to buy the record or borrow a friend's CD. The number and variety of songs that someone could obtain in this way were limited by that person's music budget and their immediate network of friends. Napster not only made music files readily available, it did so free of charge and at the click of a button, and it enabled any person connected to the Internet to obtain copies of songs from anyone else who was also connected to the Internet and using Napster.

The original version of Napster was eventually dismantled as a result of copyright infringement lawsuits brought against the company by the Recording Industry Association of America (RIAA) and others (see the section on "Metallica, Napster, and the RIAA" on page 113). In 2002, Fanning founded Snocap, a business-to-business digital music distributor, which authenticated and relicensed digital music. Snocap's 2006 partnership with Myspace allowed bands to sell their music directly through their Myspace pages for any fee they wanted, with Myspace sharing that fee with Snocap. However, the venture struggled financially, and Snocap was eventually bought by the music streaming site Imeem in 2008. Fanning's next project, Rupture, an online gaming community that builds a gamer profile with information from all the different games he or she may play, was purchased by Electronic Arts in 2008.

teacher and to the student himself or herself, that he or she has developed good research and writing skills. Students can avoid this problem by paraphrasing and writing summaries, always being sure to credit the source in the paraphrase or summary. Unique phrases that are used directly should always be included within quotation marks.

COPYRIGHT AND FAIR USE

Copyright is a form of intellectual property law that protects the authorship of original works. The types of works that are protected by U.S. copyright law include "literary, dramatic, musical, and artistic works, such as poetry, novels, movies, songs, computer software, and architecture." Copyright does not protect facts or ideas, but it may protect the expression of facts or ideas. For example, no one can copyright the idea of the history of the U.S. Civil War, but an author can copyright his or her particular book describing the history of the Civil War. In fact, many authors can have copyrights on different books they have written about the Civil War. A copyright is different from a patent, which protects discoveries and inventions.

An original work is protected by copyright as soon as it is created and put into a tangible form that can be perceived directly or with the aid of a machine or device such as a computer, movie projector, or musical instrument. For example, an essay is protected by copyright as soon as it is written on paper or stored on a computer hard disk drive, and a photograph is protected by copyright as soon as it is put on film or stored on a digital camera's memory card. A work does not have to be formally published to be covered by copyright law. The copyright protects the exclusive rights of the author for a limited time, usually during the life of the author and for 70 years from the date of the author's death. When a copyright has expired, the work is said to have entered into the public domain and can be freely used by anyone without permission of the copyright owner.

If the author of a copyrighted work has been hired to produce the work, then the copyright becomes the property of the employer. This may also be the case when a work and its copyright are purchased from an author. This is why many copyrights for books, music, and movies are owned by publishers and other companies, rather than the authors, musicians, and scriptwriters who authored the works.

Copyright infringement is the act of copying a copyright-protected work without permission of the copyright owner during the time when the copyright is still in force. In the eyes of the law, copyright infringement is equivalent to theft and is subject to civil penalties and even to criminal prosecution in some circumstances. Civil penalties for copyright infringement may be equivalent to actual losses incurred by the copyright owner as a result of the infringement. When copyright infringement is done to make a profit, it can be prosecuted as a federal crime. Criminal prosecution for copyright infringement is less common than civil actions and is currently applied most often to people who engage in large scale *pirating* of CDs, DVDs, or digital music and video files. The FBI warning that is displayed at the beginning of most movie DVDs threatens a maximum penalty of up to five years in prison and a $250,000 fine for criminal copyright infringement.

There is an exception to the prohibition against copying a copyrighted work without the permission of the author. This exception is known as fair use. Acts of copying a copyrighted work which fall within the definition of fair use do not constitute copyright infringement. As a result, the copyright owner cannot use his or her copyright to stop others from copying the work in ways that constitute fair use.

Those who are interested in making use of a copyrighted work, therefore, are very interested in knowing whether the uses they would like to make of a work constitute fair use. Unfortunately, the definition of fair use is very fuzzy and difficult to apply in particular cases. Under U.S. law, whether a particular use of a copyrighted work constitutes a fair use of the work depends on a combination of at least four factors: (1) the purpose and character of the use of the copyrighted work; (2) the nature of the copied work; (3) the amount and substantiality of copying of the copyrighted work; and (4) the effect of the copying on the potential market for or value of the copyrighted work.

Some examples may make it easier to understand what may and may not constitute fair use. Academic uses of a work, such as the showing of a portion of a copyrighted film about the U.S. Civil War by a history professor in a classroom for educational purposes, usually constitute a fair use of the film and therefore do not require permission from or payment to the owner of the film's copyright. This is because:

- the purpose and character of the use is academic, which is favored as a fair type of use under factor (1);
- the nature of the copyrighted work under factor (2) is historical fact, which is less strongly protected by copyright law than fiction;
- only a portion of the film, rather than the entire film, was shown, representing only a small amount of the copyrighted work under factor (3); and
- the showing of a portion of the film in the classroom is not likely to harm the market for the film under factor (4), because students who view a portion of the film do not become less likely to purchase or pay to rent the entire film.

As even this simple example illustrates, determining whether a particular use of a copyrighted work constitutes a fair use is very difficult because of the number of factors that need to be taken into account, the interactions among them, and the fact that no one factor dictates the outcome. For example, although uses of copyrighted works by teachers are often considered fair uses, this is not always true. A showing by a teacher of an entire feature film that has only recently been released for sale by the copyright owner might not be considered a fair use, even though such a use is academic in nature, because the other three fair use factors weigh against a finding of fair use.

Two real world cases further illustrate how fair use can be applied. In one case, the author of an unauthorized biography of the reclusive writer J. D. Salinger paraphrased large portions of unpublished letters in the biography. The letters were publically accessible at a university library, but Salinger had never authorized them for reproduction in another work. The letters made up a large portion of the biography and could be seen as being used for profit by the biographer. Salinger successfully sued and blocked publication of the biography. Fair use was found not to be applicable in this case.

In a similar case, a biographer of Richard Wright quoted from several unpublished letters and journal entries by Wright. In this case, the quotations were found to be fair use because the quoted letters and journal entries constituted less than 1 percent of Wright's unpublished work and were used for informational purposes in the biography.

The similarities between these two cases and their different outcomes illustrate how flexible the application of fair use law can be. Judgments on fair use are made in federal court, where fair use guidelines can be applied differently on a case-by-case basis. Judges in fair use cases have a large amount of freedom in deciding the outcome of each individual case. Anyone who decides to reproduce a copyrighted work, therefore, should exercise caution when assuming that fair use law will apply and that permission of the copyright holder is not required. As a result, many publishers require their authors to obtain express permission from copyright holders before including quotations from other works in their own books, even if such quotations are only a few words long and therefore extremely likely to constitute fair use, because the publishers are not willing to take on the risk that a judge might disagree.

METALLICA, NAPSTER, AND THE RIAA

When the MP3 digital format for music became popular in the late 1990s, online software services were developed that allowed people to freely share MP3 files. These services ignored copyright law and enabled the reproduction of copyrighted musical works without the permission of the copyright holder, which in most cases was a record company, artist, or group of artists. The best-known file-swapping service was Napster, discussed above. Napster was easier to use than other file-swapping services and quickly became very popular. The large number of MP3 file swaps that Napster enabled brought it to the attention of the music industry, and Napster was soon accused of copyright violations.

In late 1999, the Recording Industry Association of America (RIAA), an organization that represents a group of major record companies, filed suit against Napster for copyright infringement, alleging that the file-swapping service deprived artists and music publishers of millions of dollars in lost revenues that were protected by copyright law. Napster's defense was that its service was protected by fair use doctrine since copying was not being done for commercial gain. An additional argument was that the service should not be held accountable for any copyright infringement that was committed by users of the service. Napster also contended that its users were protected by the Audio Home Recording Act of 1992, which allows the personal copying of music and video to home recording devices. Napster claimed additionally that trying to block copyrighted files would force the 40-employee company to go out of business.

A few months later, the heavy metal band Metallica discovered that a demo of an unreleased song was being circulated on Napster and as a result had been played on radio stations. The band filed a separate suit against Napster, alleging that the service encouraged music piracy and enabled rampant copyright infringement. Included in the suit were Yale University, USC, and Indiana University. The academic institutions were being held accountable for students who used Napster on university computer networks. One month later, rapper and music producer Dr. Dre filed a similar suit.

Not all artists at that time were opposed to file-swapping services. In 2000, tracks from a new CD by the group Radiohead were leaked onto Napster three months before the scheduled release date. The band's record company panicked

(continues on page 116)

Jon Johansen (Norwegian Teenager Who Cracked the DVD Encryption Scheme and Posted the DVD-Cracking Software Online)

Jon Lech Johansen, also known as "DVD Jon," was born in Harstad, Norway, in November 1983 to a Norwegian father and Polish mother. His first computer encounter took place just a month after his birth, with his father's Sinclair ZX Spectrum. At age 12, Jon was writing simple computer programs. When Jon was 14, his father brought home a digital camera that came with less than perfect software. Jon analyzed the code and wrote an improved version, which also reduced the number of steps needed to transfer photos from 25 to just one.

At 15, Jon installed Linux for the first time but was soon frustrated by the lack of DVD support and by the need to run Windows in order to be able to play DVDs on his computer. He began working on developing DVD support for Linux in collaboration with a German and a Dutch computer programmer whom he met online. In 1999, they released DeCSS, a system that was able to crack the content scrambling system (CSS) encryption used to protect DVDs and thus make it possible to play them on a machine running Linux. The trio became known as MoRE, or Masters of Reverse Engineering. Jon posted the link to the source code of DeCSS on the Internet, and the program spread quickly among Linux users. Unlike the other members of MoRE, who chose to remain anonymous, Johansen used his real name when speaking to the media about the program. He believed that he was doing nothing wrong. Johansen received a prestigious Norwegian student merit award, the Karoline, for his contributions to DeCSS, and he accepted the Electronic Frontier Foundation Award on behalf of MoRE. At 16, he dropped out of high school to become a professional computer programmer. Shortly thereafter, he found himself indicted on charges of copyright infringement and gaining unauthorized access to data in connection with the creation of DeCSS.

The international affiliate of the Motion Picture Association of America (MPAA) contacted Johansen and requested that he remove the link to the source code from his Web site. Jon complied but reposted the link a week later after his father consulted with an attorney and became convinced that DeCSS was legal. On January 24, 2000, Norwegian authorities searched Johansen's home, seized his computers and cell phone, and Jon was taken to the police for questioning.

10011101001010101001100101110110101010101001

Computer hacker Jon Johansen speaks to the press in Oslo, Norway, in 2003 in connection with his retrial for creating software for cracking the encryption scheme on DVDs. *(Morten Holm/AFP/Getty Images)*

Johansen insisted that DeCSS was intended to make DVD playback possible on unsupported systems, such as Linux. Although DeCSS made it possible to pirate DVD protected content, copying movies was not the goal of the program, unlike other decryption programs that were geared specifically at bypassing CSS encryption in order to copy unencrypted movies. The MPAA and the DVD Copy Control Association also claimed that Johansen's program facilitated copyright infringement and cost the movie industry millions of dollars in losses due to unauthorized distribution of movies.

Jon was acquitted of all charges by the Norwegian court in January 2003. The court found no evidence that Jon was aiding piracy when he contributed to the creation of DeCSS and dismissed the unauthorized access to data charge by finding that the data in question was his own. The prosecutors appealed the decision,

(continues)

10011101001010101001100101110110101010101001

```
001101010010100111010110101010101011001010000 1
```

(continued)

but the original verdict in favor of Jon was upheld in December 2003. In 2005, Norwegian copyright law was amended, making the posting of a program that circumvents DVD encryption technology illegal.

Jon next found himself in trouble with Apple Computer in 2004, when he wrote a program that reverse-engineered FairPlay, the encryption technology Apple used to keep the songs sold through the iTunes store from being played on devices other than the iPod. Jon's motivation for the project was his dislike of closed systems that limit consumer choices by forcing them to use technologies they may not otherwise have chosen.

In 2005, Jon moved to the United States to work on a project for Michael Robertson, a tech entrepreneur and founder of mp3.com and San Diego company MP3tunes. Johansen is currently working for Double Twist, a company he started with Monique Farantzos. Johansen wrote two programs for Double Twist, one that allowed iTunes songs to be played on other devices, and one that allowed other songs to be played on the iPod. Double Twist also allows users to send video and photos to their friends on other platforms. So far Apple has not attempted legal action against Double Twist.

```
001101010010100111010110101010101011001010000 1
```

(continued from page 113)

as the songs became the most heavily shared files on Napster. Within a few days, the songs had been copied tens of thousands of times. To the record company's surprise, a week after the CD's official release it went to the top of the album charts in the United States. This was a first for a Radiohead release, and the evidence seemed to point to distribution on Napster helping rather than hurting CD sales. Some argue that this demonstrates that copying works and making music available on peer-to-peer services is not unethical because it can help the artists whose work was copied.

In February 2001, Napster had exhausted its appeals and was ordered to cease operation until it could guarantee that 100 percent of copyrighted material was blocked from being copied. Unable to satisfy this blocking requirement, Napster changed its policy and switched from an open file-sharing service to a paid subscription service that collected fees from subscribers and made payments to copyright holders. The company struggled for several years but was unable to maintain sufficient revenue from subscriptions and was eventually purchased by Best Buy in 2008.

Today, Napster is best known for raising issues related to the ethics of music sharing and for challenging the concept of music copyright protection in the digital age. Despite the legal judgment against Napster, online sharing of copyright-protected music files remains widespread because the technology of peer-to-peer file sharing developed and spread more quickly than the legal system could keep pace with it. Other free file-swapping sites have replaced Napster, and many have avoided legal action because of technical and organizational differences in how they operate. The music industry has responded by supporting services that allow digital distribution of music for a fee. The Apple iTunes music service is the most successful of these. As a practical matter, such services have largely balanced the interests of artists, publishers, and the public, and therefore lead to greater willingness of consumers to purchase songs rather than download them for free using peer-to-peer services. As a result, although the ethical questions surrounding file-sharing remain, economic developments have made such issues less pressing than they were a decade ago.

CONCLUSIONS

Authors, musicians, and artists throughout the ages have incorporated the works of others into their own works. In writing *Romeo and Juliet,* William Shakespeare borrowed heavily from the earlier Italian work *The Tragical History of Romeus and Juliet.* Many subsequent works, including the American musical *West Side Story,* have since adapted the story of Romeo and Juliet to fit modern culture. Far from plagiarism, such incorporation of themes, plots, and characters from earlier works is considered the creation of a new work, so long as the resulting adaption contains sufficient original thought. A reinterpretation of an old work can even become a classic in its own right, particularly if the new work retains the basic theme of the original work but expresses that theme using the original insights of the author and applies those insights to a new context. For example, *West Side Story* did not simply retell *Romeo and Juliet* but expressed the same tragic theme of true love between a couple from different warring groups that leads to the death of both lovers, but within a different context.

More recently, with the advent of analog and digital recording equipment, many composers and musical recording artists began to copy small portions of songs recorded by other artists into their own recordings. Such *sampling* usually copies a memorable portion of another song, such as its bass line, chorus, or drumbeat. Although sampling is most often associated with rap and hip-hop, the practice began as long ago as the 1960s. Although many at first accused those who used sampling of plagiarism and lack of creativity, sampling has become more widely accepted in recent years, particularly if the sample is used not solely to piggyback on the notoriety of the sample, but to build on the sample to create a recording that differs substantially from the original. One way in which this often is done is to take a sample from one genre of music, such as heavy metal, and to use it as the basis for a song in a different genre, such as rap or reggae.

Sampling was first performed using analog audiotapes, followed by digital audiotapes, and then computers. The same basic pattern can be found for many kinds of copying. As computer technology evolves, it creates new ways to copy the work of other's into one's own. This increased freedom does not necessarily make copying any more or less ethical. Although it is not easy to establish rules about whether particular acts of copying are permissible, a good general rule is that a new work makes ethically permissible use of an old work if the new work does not merely copy the old work without modification but instead transforms the old work to such an extent that the new work represents substantial original and creative input from the creator of the new work. To the extent that this is true, although the technological tools for copying the works of others may change, the ethical compass for guidance will generally continue to point in the same direction in the face of even the greatest technological advances.

7

SPEECH: THE INTERNET AS LIBRARY, NEWSPAPER, TELEVISION, AND BEYOND

One of the most common ways in which computers and the Internet are used is as tools for communicating. Almost every computer user today uses his or her computer to send and receive e-mail and text messages, to write and read blog postings, to stay in touch with friends using social networking sites, and to read a wide variety of information on Web sites. Professional authors, journalists, and educators use the Internet to communicate. Traditional media companies, such as radio stations and television networks, have turned to the Internet to broadcast their programs and to communicate with viewers and listeners. This chapter explores just a few of the ethical issues that arise from the use of computers and the Internet as tools for communication.

THE PERMANENCE OF INTERNET SPEECH

The Internet is the next link in a chain of communication developments that include telegraph, telephone, radio, film, and television. Each of these developments allowed human communication to transcend the limitations of time and space. The Internet stands apart from such earlier developments due to its unique features, including its immediacy, worldwide reach, and interactivity. Anyone who can access a networked computer can become an

Permanence of Internet Speech

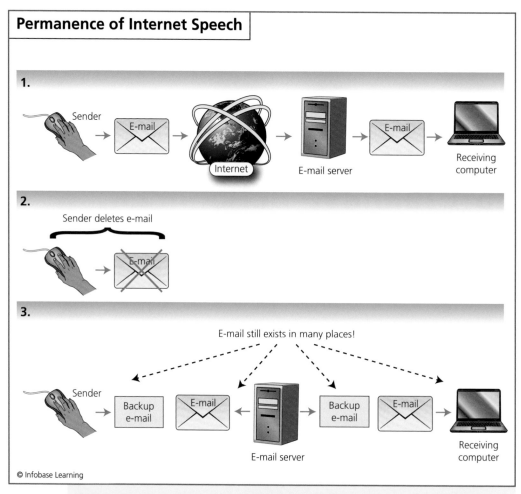

1.

Sender → E-mail → Internet → E-mail server → E-mail → Receiving computer

2.

Sender deletes e-mail

3.

E-mail still exists in many places!

Sender → Backup e-mail → E-mail → E-mail server → Backup e-mail → E-mail → Receiving computer

© Infobase Learning

Pre-Internet communications often could be deleted easily and permanently by their senders or recipients. For example, a letter written on paper and delivered by postal mail could be destroyed by its recipient, thereby removing any record that the letter ever existed. Internet communications, however, such as e-mail messages, typically are copied repeatedly and automatically at several locations along the path from sender to recipient, thereby making it difficult, if not impossible, for either the sender or recipient to eliminate all traces of the communication.

active presence on the Internet, posting information that might remain available online for a long period—perhaps as long as the Internet continues to exist. The permanence of information and the potentially widespread audience for information present unique ethical challenges to users of computers and the Internet.

For example, a personal opinion expressed to a friend or family member offline usually will not travel too far outside one's circle of acquaintances. When the same opinion is expressed in an e-mail message, blog, or online forum, it has the potential to become very public and to remain available online indefinitely. For example, if someone sends an e-mail message to even one other person, the message may be saved in multiple locations, including in the e-mail accounts of both the sender and receiver, on servers used by the Internet service providers of both the sender and receiver, and on backup drives in a variety of locations. Once the e-mail message has been sent, it can therefore take on a life of its own, causing the sender of the message to lose control over its distribution. Even if both the sender and recipient immediately delete the copies of the e-mail message on their own computers, this may not delete the additional copies of the e-mail message. If any such copy is posted to a Web site, intentionally or unintentionally, it may be further copied either manually by other users or even automatically by Web spider software, at which point it may become impossible as a practical matter to remove all copies of the e-mail message from the Internet. The message may be redistributed by others years later or even modified to change the meaning of the message.

There are a wide variety of ways to communicate online and some may be more permanent than others. However, the degree of permanence of a particular medium may not always be apparent. For example, an e-mail message sent by one person to an e-mail list may be delivered not only to the members of the list but also posted automatically to a Web page whose purpose is to serve as an archive for messages in the list. The person who sends the message may not even be aware that such a Web-based record exists. Similarly, many people may think that they own the content on social networking sites such as Facebook. However, such sites are owned by private companies that may analyze and copy certain content from users' pages, within only the relatively loose confines established by the companies themselves. There is no guarantee, for example, that if a user deactivates his or her account on a social networking site, that the information in that account will be deleted.

Cloud computing is a relatively new concept that encompasses a wide variety of Internet services. In general, the term cloud computing refers to any service that allows individuals to store data and/or software online rather than on the hard disk of the user's own computer. Netbooks and mobile phones that access the Internet are conducive to cloud computing because they do not have a significant amount of storage space. Google provides several cloud computing applications, including Gmail, Google Calendar, and Google Docs. Users of these applications gain the benefit of having their e-mail, calendar data, and documents accessible from any computer with an Internet connection. One aspect of this type of cloud computing that is perhaps not as apparent is that the data are controlled by Google and may have more permanence than data stored on an individual's computer. Furthermore, users of Google cloud applications trust that Google will maintain the security and privacy of the data that has been stored in the cloud. In reality, cloud data is beyond the control of its originator and could be deleted or copied without the owner's permission. It could also be subpoenaed by a government agency. Furthermore, the user may simply forget that he or she has a particular cloud-based account, in which case the data in that account could remain in the cloud indefinitely.

Legal protections for freedom of speech in the United States allow anyone to publish almost any type of material on the Internet. In contrast, in the past there were limited forums for personal expression in print media. If an individual wrote a newspaper article or letter to the editor of a newspaper, the publisher of the newspaper was responsible for the decency and validity of the article or letter. As a result, the editor effectively imposed limits on what could be printed, thereby restricting to some degree the harm that could be caused by false, malicious, or scandalous information. Furthermore, the reach and life span of information published in newspapers were relatively limited and short. Newspapers only reached their immediate readers, with the rare exception of academics and other researchers who might manually review archives in the future. As a result, the information contained in newspapers was effectively in circulation for only a few days after it was published. Now, however, anything published online is easily available immediately and effectively forever, because anyone who uses a search engine to find information on a topic of interest can be pointed directly to content that was written years earlier and perhaps originally intended for only a small audience.

The permanence of information on the Internet must be considered when making ethical judgments about posting content. Most people would not fault someone for making a careless comment about a family member to a friend over the telephone. Yet the same statement made in an e-mail message, a blog posting, or on a social networking site can not only reach a larger number of people but remain available online for a long period of time. Therefore, a statement made in anger in the heat of the moment, which was never intended to be heard by the person it is about, could mushroom into a significant insult that is repeated over and over again, causing not only pain to its target, but also damage to a relationship. As this example illustrates, the harm that can be caused by a comment depends not only on the content of the comment but also on the number of people who have access to the comment and the length of time during which they have access. In this way, the Internet can act like both a powerful amplifier and an echo chamber.

Therefore, although many use e-mail, text messaging, and other forms of online communication to express their feelings from moment to moment, precisely because computers make it so easy to generate such communications so quickly and frequently, ethical considerations argue in favor of thinking twice and pausing before writing anything online that could cause pain, annoyance, or embarrassment to someone else. Although many respond to this kind of concern by pointing out that they have the right to say anything they want online, ethics is concerned not with whether someone has the right to say something, but with whether it *is* right to say something. The fact that the First Amendment protects a particular statement does not mean that such a statement is not hurtful to another person.

It can be difficult to judge whether a particular message will harm someone else, particularly because the sender of a message may have limited control over how such a message is copied, forwarded, and modified by those who receive it. A very conservative ethical approach, therefore, would be never to send a message that one would not be prepared to defend if it were published in a newspaper or displayed on nationwide television news. Such a strategy, however, is probably too cautious and would prevent one from taking advantage of many of the benefits of Internet-based communication. A more balanced approach is to become thoroughly educated about the extent to which messages created using different kinds of communications technology, such a telephone calls, e-mail messages, text messages, and blog postings, can be kept private and the extent to which they can be made public, and to take reasonable steps to create such messages with controls that are appropriate to their content. For example, if one were to assume that it were ethical to share a rumor directly with a close friend in person, it might be ethical to do the same by sending an e-mail message to the same friend along with a request not to forward the message to anyone else, but it would not be ethical to post the same message to a public Web site and then to forward the link to the friend. Even if one assumed that only the friend would visit the Web site, the mere public availability of the Web site could enable people to stumble upon the Web site through search engines and other means. Therefore, for better or worse, the permanence and reach of Internet speech imposes some ethical obligation on everyone who communicates over the Internet to think about the implications of technology for the harm that can be caused by what they write.

OFFENSIVE AND EXPLICIT SPEECH ON THE INTERNET

In the context of First Amendment protection for freedom of speech, the U.S. Supreme Court has drawn no distinction between the Internet and other forms of written communication, such as books and newspapers. In 1996, the U.S. government attempted to prohibit distribution of indecent material on the Internet by enacting the Communications Decency Act (CDA). The government's primary argument in favor of the CDA was that the Supreme Court had previously upheld the regulation of indecent material on television as a way of protecting children from such content. The CDA was challenged within a few months of its enactment and was soon suspended and eventually found to be unconstitutional under the First Amendment by the Supreme Court in its 1997 decision in the case *Reno v. ACLU.* The Supreme Court based its conclusion in part on the fact that government regulation of content on television was justified by the small number of channels available for television broadcasts. Because no such limitation exists on the Internet, the same justification for government regulation does not apply to Internet speech.

The Internet has provided people with an unprecedented ability to express themselves on a wide variety of topics and to reach a worldwide audience. Individuals can exchange ideas with people from all over the world. The Internet has created a global community where discussion can take place in an open forum. The freedom of discussion that the Internet allows pertains to all types of information, including material that is offensive to many people. The legality of offensive material on the Internet, however, does not necessarily imply that it is ethical to post such material.

Consider the case of a New York State eighth-grader named Aaron Wisniewski. In 2001, Aaron was suspended from school for a full semester when school administrators found out that his AOL instant messaging buddy icon consisted of a gun firing at a man's head and the caption "Kill Mr. VanderMolen," the name of one of Aaron's teachers. The icon had been transmitted to at least 15 other students from Aaron's home computer before being reported to school officials. Following Aaron's suspension, his parents sued the school district for his reinstatement. A federal court upheld the suspension, ruling that the icon constituted an on-campus threat and was not protected by law as free speech. If Aaron had made the threat in a conversation with friends, the effect probably would not have been as serious as it was when he used the Internet to transmit it. Even if the court had overruled the suspension and found that the student's speech was protected by law, this would not necessarily imply that using the icon was ethical. The law of free speech and ethics do not always coincide.

The anonymous nature of the Internet sets it apart from other forms of communication such as broadcast and print media. Opinions can be expressed anonymously or under an alias on Web sites with little fear of exposure or retribution. Although some blogs and social networking sites may attempt to censor messages posted by members, a private Web site can be used to post almost any type of information. The Internet allows the wide dissemination of hate speech toward religions, racial groups, and lifestyles. Violent acts and terrorism can be encouraged and photos of accidents and crime scenes can be posted. The Internet is available to children and young adults who may be disturbed or influenced by things they see and read on the Internet. Therefore, even if an adult posts offensive or otherwise disturbing material on the Internet with the intent solely for other adults to access such material, this may not in fact prevent children from finding such material. Furthermore, adults who would rather not encounter such material may do so inadvertently by clicking on a link or entering a query into a search engine. Certain text, images, and videos are so disturbing that even viewing them briefly can be unsettling and difficult to forget. This raises the question whether those who post content on the Internet that could be considered offensive, indecent, disturbing, or addictive have any ethical obligation to limit access to these materials to those who intentionally seek it out or at least to provide appropriate warnings so that people have an opportunity to choose to look the other way.

Before the Internet existed, the U.S. government attempted to exercise censorship over morally objectionable printed materials. Until the mid-20th century, it was illegal to print or distribute sexually explicit materials in the United States. In the 1930s, the merit of materials as varied as a sex education pamphlet written by birth control activist Mary Ware Dennett and James Joyce's landmark novel *Ulysses* were argued in federal courts. In the 1970s, the U.S. Supreme Court ruled that local communities could define obscenity and set standards for censorship. Although there is merit in allowing the definition of obscenity to vary from community to community, such an approach has been rendered moot by the Internet, since content written anywhere is instantly accessible in all communities. If a single community with a highly restrictive definition of obscenity could prohibit speech considered obscene under its own definition from being published on the Internet, then the Internet would be limited to containing content that satisfied the most-restrictive community's standard of obscenity.

When the federal government got out of the censorship business, entertainment industries instituted limited forms of self-censorship. For example, the Motion Picture Association of America (MPAA) and the National Association of Theater Owners instituted the ratings system that judges films for elements such as language, nudity, and violence and applies a rating to each film. The rating system can be used by parents to help decide which movies are appropriate for their children to see. Before the advent of cable television, the major networks censored the material they broadcast. When cable broadcasting became popular, many of the taboos related to television disappeared. In response to pressure from cable subscribers, most cable systems began to provide support for parental control by providing a way for parents to block certain content from their cable system. Another example of self-censorship is the rating system used by the Recording Industry Association of America (RIAA). A parental advisory label is applied to warn parents about music that contains explicit lyrics. All of these mechanisms are provided to help parents who want to apply their personal ethics to the content they allow their children to see.

Limiting access to certain content on the Internet has proved to be more difficult to enforce. Unlike a movie theater, which can refuse to sell tickets to adult movies to children, the operator of a Web site cannot positively verify the age of visitors to that Web site. As a result, very few Web sites that contain explicit or offensive content attempt to restrict access to content, except possibly by requiring the user to verify his or her age by providing a birth date, which is not possible for the Web site to verify.

Furthermore, as mentioned above, it is possible to accidentally stumble upon an offensive Web site while surfing the Web, and many unethical Web site operators take advantage of this by using a practice known as *typosquatting* to trick Internet users into viewing their Web sites. Typosquatting, also known as *URL hijacking,* is accomplished by registering a Web site address (URL) that is slightly different from a popular Web site, with the goal of catching users who make typographical errors when typing a URL into their Web browser's address bar. Some typosquatting is prohibited by law, and some Web site owners attempt to prevent typosquatting by registering misspelled versions of their own domain names.

Milwaukee police lead comedian George Carlin off the Summerfest Grounds in Milwaukee, Wisconsin, in 1972 after he allegedly used profane language during his act. *(AP Images)*

Malicious e-mail messages can also be used to fool Internet users into visiting offensive Web sites, by including links that appear to point to legitimate Web sites but instead point to Web sites containing pornography, get-rich-quick schemes, or viruses. Even some reputable Web sites sell advertising space in the form of pop-up windows and banners that may contain offensive images. For parents who want to shield their children from objectionable content, the only solution currently available is to buy third-party filtering software that limits

Internet access to a set of approved sites. The burden of censoring Internet content is on the parent. This is in contrast to earlier censorship mechanisms, such as movie ratings system and parental controls on cable television, that were supplied by the content provider.

The decentralized nature of the Internet has discouraged the establishment of a universal rating system. The most popular Web sites that allow members to post content, such as YouTube and Facebook, have guidelines that prohibit the posting of sexually explicit content, hate speech, and other offensive content. These Web sites also police new content and censor it when it is in violation of the published guidelines, but the sheer quantity of new content makes it difficult to enforce these policies consistently and quickly. Many religious organizations and education institutions have created guidelines for the ethical use of the Internet, but there are currently no established standards or mechanisms to protect children and adult Internet users from exposure to offensive online material. The Internet is often compared to the Wild West, where lawlessness and mistrust were rampant. In the absence of a sheriff to police the Internet, individual users must protect themselves and their children from offensive content.

Search engines such as Google and Yahoo recognize that many people do not want their search results to include adult sites that contain explicit material. This group of people includes both parents who want to shield their children and adults who would rather not see such material. It may also include business owners who want to restrict employee exposure to explicit materials at work. In response, most search engines now provide users with the option to filter out adult content and other types of objectionable content.

There are several other popular mechanisms for filtering Web site content. Many Internet service providers (ISPs) provide built-in filtering tools that can be used to restrict access to explicit Web sites. An example is AT&T's Smart Limits, which can be tailored to adjust filtering for different family members using the same computer. There are also hardware routers that allow different filtering levels to be set for different users of a computer. Netgear's Security Edition is an example of a router with filtering capabilities. Recognizing the demand for content filtering, several personal computer operating systems have built-in support for filtering. Both Windows 7 and the Mac OS provide suites of parental control features.

`100111010010101010011001011101101010100101001`

Ashcroft v. Free Speech Coalition

The U.S. Supreme Court has held that pornography produced using children is not protected by the First Amendment right to free speech. The Child Pornography Prevention Act (CPPA) of 1996 went one step farther by prohibiting not only pornographic images that represent actual children, but also films, pictures, or computer-generated images that depict what *appears* to be a child involved in sexual acts. Such *virtual child pornography* could include, for example, computer-generated images of children or animated drawings of children. One argument that influenced Congress to enact the CPPA was that virtual child pornography might incite pedophiles to abuse children. The broad nature of the CPPA, however, was seen by many as encroaching on First Amendment free speech guarantees. The case *Ashcroft v. Free Speech Coalition* challenged the premise that the production and possession of pornography that only appears to involve children is illegal, even when no actual children were used in its production.

The prohibition against virtual child pornography was initially upheld by a U.S. District Court. On appeal, the Ninth Circuit Court of Appeals reversed this ruling and found that free speech cannot be limited just because it encourages people to engage in illegal activities and that the original justification for prohibiting child pornography was that real children were hurt during its production. The U.S. Supreme Court subsequently reviewed the ruling and agreed with the decision of the Ninth Circuit Court of Appeals, ruling that the First Amendment pertains to words rather than deeds and does not prohibit words on the basis of the deeds they may encourage. As a result, the law in the United States remains that pornography that is produced using children is not protected as free speech under the First Amendment but pornography that merely appears to depict children, but whose production did not involve real children, can still be protected as free speech under the First Amendment.

`100111010010101010011001011101101010100101001`

All of these filter mechanisms allow Internet users to take control over the content they view and to exercise their personal ethics and preferences to decide what type of information they will be exposed to on the Internet.

PUTTING PUBLICLY AVAILABLE INFORMATION ONLINE

Like text and photographs that are published in books, newspapers, and magazines, content that has been posted on the Internet is subject to copyright protection. Posting content that belongs to someone else can result in charges of copyright infringement. However, posting information that is already in the public domain is perfectly legal. The question remains, however, whether posting public domain information on the Internet could ever be unethical.

As an example, imagine an adult who uses Facebook for professional networking. One day he finds that embarrassing pictures from his high school yearbook have been posted and tagged with his name. Since the pictures have already been published in a yearbook they are publicly available, but posting them on a Facebook page makes them available to a wider audience and possibly gives them more permanence. The students who originally posed for the pictures had no idea they would ever be seen by anyone outside of their families and high school friends. The ethical issue of control over content is also relevant in this example, since no one can delete the pictures or the tags except the person who posted them. While there is nothing illegal about posting the pictures, there is the possibility of hurting the reputation of people depicted in the pictures. Since the pictures can hurt other people, it may not be ethical to post them.

This issue takes on a wider scope when public figures are considered. For example, the tax returns of judges, legislators, and state governors are already available to the public. However, obtaining copies of such documents can take a fair amount of effort. As a result, few people attempt to obtain access to such records. The effect is that although the tax returns of public officials are technically publicly available, in practice they remain relatively private. Now imagine that links to the tax records of judges are posted directly on the home pages of court Web sites. In one sense, this does not make the tax records any more public than they were before. However, the new links do make it easier for members of the public to obtain the records and perhaps even more likely that members of the public will consider obtaining such records, because they will be more likely to come across the links when visiting the court Web sites. On one hand, providing such information about public officials can be seen as enabling the public to make decisions about public affairs, particularly if the judges are elected by

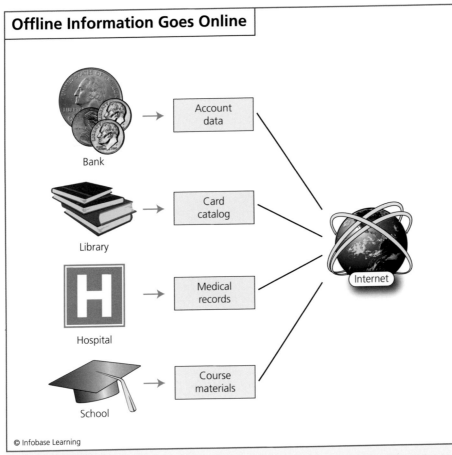

Offline Information Goes Online

Bank → Account data

Library → Card catalog

Hospital → Medical records

School → Course materials

Internet

© Infobase Learning

Information that was previously available offline in paper records, such as bank records, library card catalogs, medical records, and university course materials, increasingly are being made available online. Such movement of data to the online world may not raise ethical issues if sufficient controls over access to the online information are put in place. However, ethical issues can arise if making information available online can lead to privacy violations or security breaches that were unlikely to occur with offline material.

the public. On the other hand, the judges have a reasonable concern that making their tax records highly public, rather than merely public, crosses a line into invading their privacy, particularly if the records provide evidence of alimony payments, poor investment decisions, or other actions that are lawful but potentially embarrassing to the judge. Such information may or may not be relevant to the judge's ability to serve the public faithfully.

A view of a street in Manchester, England, with a laptop computer showing the same street on Google Maps Street View. The increasing availability of street-level images online is raising questions about protection of individual privacy, especially when such images display private homes and faces of individual people. *(Tim Meyers/Alamy)*

As a final example, consider the posting of blueprints for power plants, water treatment facilities, and other critical public utilities online. Even though the plans are publicly available through a government agency, posting them online could make them more readily available to terrorists. Having to obtain such plans by visiting an agency in person and reviewing them on a desk in a room might deter a terrorist or at least make him easier to catch after the fact. Many claim that this is a compelling argument for not making such information easily available online. On the other hand, making such information publicly available might help the local community understand the utilities in their area and possibly address problems with these facilities, including security problems. This problem has caused particular controversy since the terrorist attacks on September 11, 2001, and likely will require additional debate before any degree of agreement is reached on how best to balance public safety with the public interest in obtaining information about how public facilities operate.

CITIZEN WATCHDOG VIDEOS

In 1991, a bystander videotaped four white Los Angeles police officers beating an African American suspected of drunk driving named Rodney King. The video footage received extensive coverage on local and national news programs. The four LAPD officers were subsequently tried and acquitted of assaulting King. In large part due to evidence seen in the videotape, the outcome of the trial sparked outrage. Six days of rioting in Los Angeles followed, resulting in millions of dollars in property damage and the deaths of 53 people. The new era of citizen surveillance of police had begun.

By the end of the 1990s, television broadcasts of citizen videos of police actions had become commonplace. The videos were usually filmed with portable VHS video cameras. Most people did not carry around these cameras, so the filming usually occurred when someone had the time to retrieve a camera or happened to have a camera in their car. In recent years, cell phone cameras have led to an explosion in the number of people who have filmed police actions. Instead of sending video footage to news programs, citizen watchdogs can now upload it to a video-sharing site like YouTube. By the time new programs show footage of a police action, it often has already gone viral online.

Cell phones and the Internet give each citizen the power to become a journalist and activist, chronicling police misbehavior and broadcasting it to the world. A search of the Internet reveals stories from across the country of people who have been found innocent of falsified charges following the posting of a citizen video. Technology is allowing citizens to expose government and police corruption, and the Internet is serving as the new free press.

Many law enforcement agencies have started to enforce existing wiretapping and eavesdropping laws in an attempt to limit the filming of police actions. A motorcyclist in Maryland named Anthony Graber who surreptitiously filmed a traffic stop was charged with illegal wiretapping. Maryland is one of 12 states with laws that require both parties to consent to the recording of a private conversation. The case was dismissed, but Graber could have been sentenced to 16 years in prison.

There are also cases in which citizen videos can work in favor of law enforcement officers involved in violent incidents. In 2009, a confrontation between a white Oakland transit officer named Johannes Mehserle and Oscar Grant, an unarmed African-American train passenger, was filmed by several witnesses. The footage was immediately posted on the Internet and led to violent protests that were an echo of the Rodney King riots. Due to civil unrest in Oakland, Mehserle was tried for murder in Los Angeles. In his defense, Mehserle claimed he thought he was using a stun gun on Grant but had mistakenly unholstered his revolver. Video from several witnesses supported Mehserle's story and showed his emotional reaction after the shooting, resulting in his conviction for the lesser charge of manslaughter.

CONCLUSIONS

The explosion in the use of computers and the Internet as tools for communication and personal expression shows no signs of stopping. In fact, the proliferation of handheld mobile devices with broadband Internet connections and the ability to browse the Web and send and receive voice calls, e-mail messages, and text messages likely means that people will continue to communicate with a larger and more varied audience even more frequently than ever before in coming years. Perhaps the incredibly rapid speed with which methods of communication are expanding and changing is leading to a gap between the way in which people experience Internet-based communication and the way in which such communication actually works. Tapping out a message on Twitter can feel like a highly personal act, no different from writing a note to a friend, and yet the resulting tweet may be readable by thousands of other people. Conversely, one might feel like a famous author, writing for an audience of millions, when writing a blog posting that in reality is read by only a few people.

Such technological developments and the ways in which people experience them do not fit neatly within previously existing categories of communication, such as face-to-face communication, newspaper publishing, or making a speech. Instead, communication using computers and the Internet takes a much wider variety of forms that blend various qualities of the old forms and also take on new features. Therefore, although it is possible to look at the ethical guideposts and conclusions derived from older forms of communication relating to notions such as decency, slander, and etiquette, it will likely be necessary to tailor such concepts to the particular characteristics of new media so that human communication can continue to flourish without causing intentional or unintentional harm to others through words.

8

NETIQUETTE: ADDING FORMALITY TO AN INFORMAL MEDIUM

Internet technology allows people to connect. E-mail, blogs, social networking Web sites, and online forums have created new ways for people to meet, stay in touch, and conduct business. The term *etiquette* refers to the conventions and courtesies that govern social interaction. New modes of online communication have led to the development of some new conventions and a new term has been adopted to describe them—netiquette. This chapter will focus on the evolving conventions of netiquette.

Online communication methods share some unique characteristics. In general, writing on the Internet is less formal than writing that appears in print media such as books, newspapers, and magazines. Print articles typically have a title and follow a thought-out structure of sections, paragraphs, and sentences. Rules of grammar are strictly followed and slang is avoided. Formal names are used when discussing people. In contrast, writing on the Internet is often done quickly and without strict adherence to structure or language usage. Slang and questionable language abound. Although there are some online articles that resemble printed articles, writing done for blogs and social networking sites such as Facebook and Twitter tends to be spontaneous and casual. This type of writing often relies on shorthand in the form of acronyms and emoticons to convey meaning.

The conventions of social etiquette include rules for writing correspondence. The most formal type of letters include a header with the date and addresses of the sender and receiver, a formal salutation (such as "Dear Ms. Smith"), a body, and a respectful closing (such as "Sincerely") that includes a handwritten signature. Grammar and punctuation are critically important in a formal letter. E-mail messages, in contrast, often dispense with capitalization, grammar, and punctuation. A salutation may consist of just a name (for example, "Jim") or it may be left out altogether. The closing may be shortened or omitted, since the receiver knows who sent the e-mail message.

Looking back at the history of written communication, it can be seen that messages that required more time to compose and send were usually more formal. When letters were delivered in a wagon pulled by horses or carried across the ocean in a ship, senders took time to carefully craft and write their letters. A letter that took weeks to be delivered had to make its message perfectly clear and leave as few questions as possible about its intent, because providing clarification to the recipient required such a significant amount of time and effort.

As more frequent and easier communication passes between two people, either face-to-face or written, there is a tendency for the communication to become more informal. There are many benefits to informal communication, both socially and in the business world. It builds relationships between people and adds a human touch that may be lacking in formal communication. When face-to-face or phone contact is not possible due to constraints of time and space, informal online communication can bridge the gap.

Instant messages, texts, and tweets are the most informal type of online writing. They are unique since they represent instantaneous written communication that is not available in any other medium. These quick written messages have developed their own conventions for compressing meaning into as few words as possible. These conventions will be discussed later in this chapter.

THE NEED FOR NETIQUETTE

Many of the rules of etiquette are based on common sense, which is also true of the rules of netiquette. People who use the Internet on a regular basis usually become aware of the unspoken rules of good manners online, while those who are unaware of the conventions may come across as rude or uneducated. When someone shows a lack of online savvy, they should be treated with the same courtesy and patience as someone who is unaware of social etiquette. Showing respect to other people while online is the best way to make the rules of netiquette common practice and ensure that most people have a good experience when using the Internet.

E-mail has become an immensely popular form of communication and in some cases has replaced the telephone and letter for both social and business communication. One of the drawbacks of e-mail compared to face-to-face contact and even telephone conversations is the absence of nonverbal cues such as tone of voice, facial expressions, and body language. The words in an e-mail message carry more weight since they must communicate all of the meaning of the message. Informal e-mail messages are often written quickly with words not carefully chosen. A comment that is intended to be funny might be interpreted by the recipient as an insult, or *sarcasm* may be misconstrued as anger. The lack of verbal cues in e-mail has led to the development of emoticons to help convey meaning. Emoticons are described in more detail in the next section.

Since e-mail messages are now being used for all types of communication, setting the correct tone is important. A business e-mail should follow a different set of rules than an e-mail between two close friends or family members. Correct grammar and sentence structure are more important in a business e-mail or in an e-mail to someone who is not a close friend. A formal e-mail should resemble a letter and make use of a salutation (i.e., "Dear James" or "James"), while informal e-mail messages often dispense with the salutation. Including a subject line with an e-mail message is a polite way to let the recipient know what the message is about and is useful for future reference if the message is saved. E-mails that lack subject lines or with generic subject lines such as "Hello" or "Important Information" are less useful to the recipient and can be viewed as rude because they are less respectful of the recipient's time.

In the e-mail world, overusing capital letters, question marks, and explanation points (LIKE THIS??!!) are interpreted by many as the equivalent of shouting. This is a mistake often made by new e-mail users. Another mistake is to get carried away with forwarding chain letters, cute pictures, and funny videos through e-mail. Many people consider this type of e-mail to be spam and are not appreciative of having it forwarded to them. Also, some forwarded e-mail messages may include attachments that contain viruses or malware or misinformation of the urban legend variety. When in doubt, do not forward this type of e-mail.

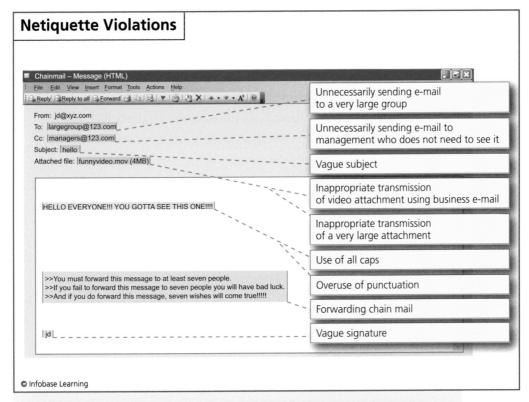

Netiquette Violations

Chainmail – Message (HTML)	
File Edit View Insert Format Tools Actions Help	Unnecessarily sending e-mail to a very large group
From: jd@xyz.com	
To: largegroup@123.com	Unnecessarily sending e-mail to management who does not need to see it
Cc: managers@123.com	
Subject: hello	Vague subject
Attached file: funnyvideo.mov (4MB)	Inappropriate transmission of video attachment using business e-mail
HELLO EVERYONE!!! YOU GOTTA SEE THIS ONE!!!!	Inappropriate transmission of a very large attachment
	Use of all caps
>>You must forward this message to at least seven people.	Overuse of punctuation
>>If you fail to forward this message to seven people you will have bad luck.	
>>And if you do forward this message, seven wishes will come true!!!!!	Forwarding chain mail
jd	Vague signature

© Infobase Learning

E-mail messages often violate the norms of netiquette, thereby causing confusion, annoyance, and frustration on the part of those who receive them. The e-mail message shown here violates commonly accepted rules of netiquette in a large number of ways. By avoiding these and other netiquette violations, those who send e-mail messages can become more effective at communicating and avoid offending those on the receiving end of such messages.

In 1995, an Intel engineer named Sally Hambridge authored a paper called *Netiquette Guidelines*. Although some of the items covered in this paper have become dated (for example, Ms. Hambridge was concerned about people sending long e-mail messages since Internet access was paid for by the minute), most of the suggestions are surprisingly timely. Here are a few of her suggestions that continue to be valuable:

- Respect copyright laws of material that you post online.
- Do not change the wording of text that you forward or post.
- Be conservative in what you send or post. Avoid sending heated messages, or *flaming*.

⊕ Consider time zones when sending e-mail. Do not expect an immediate reply if it is the middle of the night in the recipient's location.

⊕ Take into account cultural differences in language, humor, and especially sarcasm when sending e-mails or posting. Remember that a
human being with feelings will be reading it.

⊕ Also remember that there is a large audience for posts that may
include your present or future employer. Exercise caution in what
you write.

EMOTICONS, ALLCAPS, AND LOLs: A USER'S GUIDE

In the absence of facial expressions and nonverbal cues to convey one's state
of mind in an e-mail or forum post, a kind of emotional shorthand has been
created. This shorthand allows people to convey their feelings with a few
keystrokes. This section is an informal user's guide to this set of shorthand
images.

Emoticons

Emoticon is a portmanteau, a blending of the two words of *emote* and *icon*. In
the digital world, emoticon refers to a series of keystrokes that represent a picture. Most often, the representation is of a face viewed sideways. Emoticons are
used to express the writer's mood or reaction. They are sometimes used to down-
play a comment that may sound angry or complaining or to give the reader a
clue about how to interpret a sarcastic or ironic statement. Emoticons are often
referred to as modern day hieroglyphics.

COMMON EMOTICONS	
:) :-) :>	Smile
:(:-(	Frown
;) ;-)	Wink
:o :-o	Shocked, surprised
:s	Confused, embarrassed
:D	Large grin

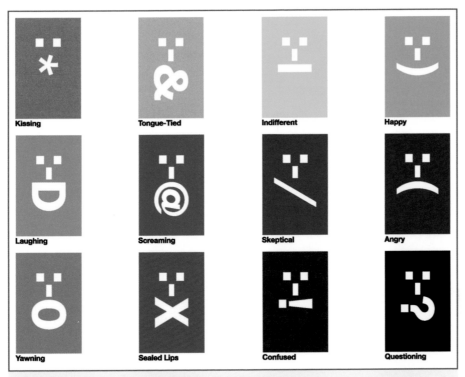

Kissing	Tongue-Tied	Indifferent	Happy
Laughing	Screaming	Skeptical	Angry
Yawning	Sealed Lips	Confused	Questioning

It can be difficult to express emotions and attitudes in e-mail and text messages. As a result, recipients of such messages sometimes misinterpret them, which can lead to confusion and even to hurt feelings. In response, emoticons, also known as smileys, were developed to make it easier to convey feelings. Emoticons are constructed from simple text characters to create images that resemble human faces (when viewed sideways) to convey emotions. The set of emoticons shown here is just a small sample of those that have evolved for use on the Internet.   *(Gary Blakeley/Shutterstock)*

While emoticons can be used to add a clever touch to an informal message, they are not appropriate in every type of message. Unless the receiver is well known, it is not a good idea to add them to formal communications. One of the negative aspects of emoticons is that they can make newcomers to the Internet feel excluded or confused.

ALLCAPS

ALLCAPS refers to using all capital letters in text. In an informal message between friends, this can be an acceptable way to put emphasis on something

001101010010100111010110101010101011001010000

Is "txt" Ruining the English Language?

Texting by cell phone is the most private and immediate form of communication enabled by new technology. The sender of a text message usually expects a quick response, which is one reason why this form of communication is more popular than e-mail or phone calls among teenagers and young adults. Groups of friends can be instantly accessible to each other through texting. As proof of the popularity of this form of communication, a 2010 Nielsen survey found that the average teenager sends 3,300 text messages per month.

Many critics of texting say this form of communication is a distraction, taking young people's focus away from school, homework, and jobs. Another criticism is that juggling several text conversations at once contributes to a shortened attention span. There is also concern that some teenagers are becoming chronically sleep deprived because they wake up during the night to send and receive text messages.

One of the most widespread criticisms of texting is that many users of this technology have adopted an abbreviated form of writing. Words shortened to the bare minimum (such as "r u" for "are you") and acronyms (such as "POS" for "parent over shoulder") are used extensively. Some educators and commentators see the texting shorthand as an assault on the English language. In a book appropriately titled *Txtng: The GR8 DB8,* author John Crystal quotes a British TV presenter named John Humphreys who describes texters as "vandals doing to our language what Genghis Khan did to his neighbors 800 years ago." Crystal also quotes author John Sutherland as saying, "Texting is bleak, bald, sad shorthand which masks dyslexia, poor spelling, and mental laziness."

Crystal, who is an honorary professor of linguistics at the University of Wales, disagrees with charges that texting is ruining the English language. In

001101010010100111010110101010101011001010000

or to convey a sense of sarcasm. Using all capitals is seen by experienced Internet users as the equivalent of shouting or trying to gain attention, so the practice should be limited to one's circle of friends. When ALLCAPS are used in an online forum or business e-mail, it conveys a sense of anger and excitability. It also indicates that the writer does not appear to be confident that effective rhetoric is the best way to make a point and therefore is seen as amateurish.

his book, he suggests that frequent texting is actually improving the literary skills of texters rather than eroding them and provides some evidence to support this belief. Andrea Lunsford, a professor of writing and rhetoric at Stanford University, conducted a study of student writing from 2001 to 2006, collecting more than 14,000 student writing samples from class assignments, journals, e-mail messages, and blog posts. The conclusion of the Stanford Study of Writing project was that we are actually in the midst of a literacy revival, with young people producing more writing for a more public audience than at any other time in history.

The students in Lunsford's study did 38 percent of their writing outside the classroom, something unheard of even a generation ago. The study found that most students were expert at using the correct tone for the audience of their writing. Although they used a casual tone in their online writing and texting, they were able to switch to academic-style writing for essays and term papers.

On the other hand, such studies do not address whether frequent texting, combined with decreased reading of books and writing of long-form essays by students, is eroding the attention spans of young people and failing to train them to engage in the kind of deep, sustained thought that is necessary to write a novel or conceive a truly original idea. It is a logical leap to start from the premise that today's students write short text messages more frequently than their predecessors and draw the conclusion that the current generation's writing skills therefore are improving in general. It is possible that writing frequent text messages only improves one's skill at writing text messages, just as running a mile every day for a year does not necessarily prepare one to run a marathon. Only time will tell whether increased volume of writing in short bursts necessarily leads to increased skill at expressing ideas more generally.

LOLs

Acronyms (or initialisms) are often used online to informally convey a reaction or emotion. These acronyms are a form of slang and are perfectly acceptable for informal communication between friends. The most widely used acronyms and their meanings are circulated by word of mouth on the Internet. Like emoticons, these acronyms should not be used in formal communications. Even in informal communications, some consideration should be given to their use since they can leave the uninitiated feeling excluded.

The following is a list of some of the most commonly used acronyms and their meanings:

TMI—too much information
LOL—laughing out loud
ROTFL—rolling on the floor laughing
FYI—for your information
BTW—by the way
IMHO—in my humble opinion
BFN—bye for now

BE CAREFUL WHEN FORWARDING AND REPLYING

The ability to quickly send an e-mail message is one of the greatest benefits of the Internet. It can also lead to problems for individual e-mail users. There are a variety of relatively common e-mail mistakes that can cause embarrassment, annoyance, or even the loss of a job or friend. Being aware of these mistakes and operating with a think-before-you-send frame of mind is the safest way to use e-mail.

It is relatively easy to send an e-mail message to the wrong person, and the consequences can range from humorous to embarrassing. Many e-mail applications have an auto-complete feature that finishes an e-mail address as the user types, substituting a recently used address. An e-mail message can be inadvertently sent to the wrong person by hitting send before checking the address. This can cause a problem if the message is private or confidential. Some people have had the embarrassing experience of writing an e-mail with criticism of another person and then carelessly typing in that person's address and hitting send. Both of these situations can be avoided by checking the "To" address before sending the e-mail.

Many people use a group capability to assign an alias name to a group of e-mail addresses for convenience when sending e-mails. For example, "MarketingDepartment" could be assigned as an alias for 20 individual e-mail addresses belonging to the staff of a marketing department. When a group alias is used, the e-mail addresses should be verified on a regular basis to make sure they are still appropriate. Imagine the situation where someone is fired from the company but still able to receive confidential e-mails because their home e-mail address is included in the group alias.

Other problems can occur when forwarding e-mail messages. Most e-mail applications include the text of the original e-mail message that is being forwarded. Before forwarding a message, check the included text to make sure it will not cause embarrassment or pain to anyone. Many people have made the mistake of forwarding what was meant to be a personal message. For example, imagine two coworkers named Kyle and Alex who are discussing an upcoming meeting in e-mail. Kyle makes some insulting remarks about the manager who called the meeting. Alex wonders what time the meeting is and forwards the e-mail message to the manager with the question about the time, forgetting Kyle's remarks that are part of the included text. This situation could have been avoided by deleting the included text before forwarding the message.

The decision on whether to use "Reply" or "Reply All" can also be an important one. As an example, imagine a manager sending coworkers John and Jane an e-mail message to congratulate them on a recent project. John responds to the message, letting the manager know that Jane had not done her share of the work. Unfortunately, John uses "Reply All" and includes Jane in his response.

Use of "Reply All" should be minimized out of courtesy since it can fill other people's e-mail in-boxes with unnecessary messages. Before hitting "Reply All," ask yourself whether every person who received the original e-mail really needs to see your reply. If not, then remove some of the e-mail addresses or use "Reply" instead of "Reply All." However, if limiting your reply causes a problem by creating a new e-mail "branch" or by offending those who have been left off, then "Reply All" should be used.

One of the biggest mistakes that can be made with e-mail is composing and sending a message while in an emotional state. It is always a good idea to cool off before writing an emotional e-mail message and to consider addressing the issue by phone or face-to-face. An e-mail message is more permanent than a conversation and can be forwarded to other people, putting the sender in a bad light.

Most people have regretted sending an e-mail at some point, whether due to inappropriate content, the wrong e-mail address, or some other mistake. The software designers at Google recognized this problem and added a feature known as Undo Send to the Gmail application. When this feature is turned on,

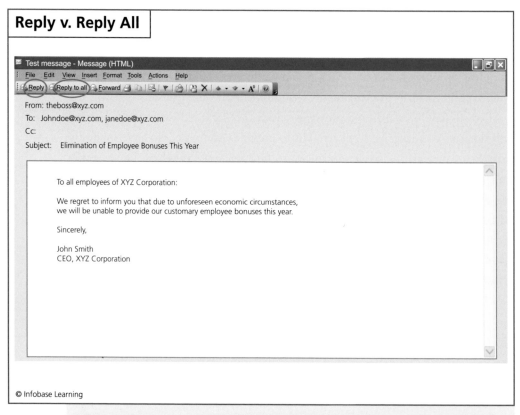

Reply v. Reply All

Test message - Message (HTML)

File   Edit   View   Insert   Format   Tools   Actions   Help

Reply   Reply to all   Forward   ▼   X   ◆ ▾ ◆ ▾ A²   ©

From: theboss@xyz.com

To: Johndoe@xyz.com, janedoe@xyz.com

Cc:

Subject: Elimination of Employee Bonuses This Year

To all employees of XYZ Corporation:

We regret to inform you that due to unforeseen economic circumstances, we will be unable to provide our customary employee bonuses this year.

Sincerely,

John Smith
CEO, XYZ Corporation

© Infobase Learning

When replying to an e-mail message, it is possible to reply either to the sender of the message by hitting the "Reply" button or to reply to both the sender and to all recipients of the message by hitting the "Reply All" button. Hitting the "Reply All" button accidentally, thereby sending a message intended only for a single person to a large number of people, can cause significant embarrassment to the sender. This mistake, however, is easy to make because the "Reply" and "Reply All" buttons resemble each other closely and typically are located adjacent to each other in e-mail software.

e-mail messages are held for a few seconds after the Send button is hit. An Undo Send button is displayed, giving the user a chance to cancel the e-mail transmission. After the delay period has elapsed, the e-mail is automatically sent.

Many e-mail messages sent late at night are regretted the next morning, especially after an evening of drinking. Gmail has another feature that addresses this problem. When the Mail Goggles function is turned on, it will monitor e-mails at designated times (such as late at night on the weekend). Before an

(continues on page 148)

`11001110100101010101001100101110110101010101001`

Scott Fahlman (The First Person to Use the Sideways Smiley Face Emoticon)

Born in 1948 in Medina, Ohio, Scott Fahlman holds a B.S. and an M.S. in electrical engineering and computer science (1973), as well as a Ph.D. in artificial intelligence from the Massachusetts Institute of Technology (1977). While at MIT, Fahlman was involved with several artificial intelligence projects, including the NETL knowledge system developed for his Ph.D. thesis. NETL stored information in a parallel network of simple hardwire elements and was able to carry out humanlike retrieval tasks. Fahlman is also one of the principal designers of the Common Lisp language. Artificial intelli-

Scott Fahlman, widely believed to be the first person to use a smiley face emoticon in an e-mail message   *(AP Images)*

gence remains Fahlman's primary research interest, and he is currently working on Scone, a system that contains large amounts of information and is able to perform humanlike searches through this information. Scone is partly based on Fahlman's earlier NETL system, but unlike NETL, Scone runs on a standard high-end workstation and does not require specialized hardware.

Fahlman arrived at Carnegie Mellon University in Pittsburg in 1978 as a research computer scientist. At the time, Carnegie Mellon's computer science community relied heavily on online bulletin boards, which were predecessors of today's newsgroups. Bulletin boards were used for all kinds of conversations between faculty, staff, and students, from somber discussions, information requests, and lost-and-found to more passionate subjects, such as politics and campus parking. Oftentimes, the humor and sarcasm of postings did not reach the reader over the bulletin board posting, provoking an angry response or resulting in hurt feelings, which would in turn cause more and more responses. Some

(continues)

`11001110100101010101001100101110110101010101001`

001101010010100111010110101010101011001010000 1

(continued)

of the users thought it might be a good idea to mark humorous posts in some way that would indicate to the reader that they are not to be taken seriously. The markers were limited by the relatively primitive nature of computer graphics of the day and had to be pretty simplistic. Some users proposed the bucket "_/", or "#" to indicate a joke. Fahlman suggested that humorous posts be marked with a ":-)" and serious-minded posts with ":-(." The notation quickly caught on, although the ":-(" eventually morphed into a sad, rather than serious face. It soon spread to other universities and research labs as scientists left Carnegie Mellon and moved elsewhere. Within a few months, lists of smileys expressing different moods began to surface: cool smileys, open-mouthed smileys, raspberry-blowing smileys. In 1993, O'Reilly & Associates published a 93-page emoticon dictionary titled *Smileys,* detailing Ronald Reagan smileys, Charlie Chaplin smileys, drooling smileys, and so on. Fahlman's bulletin board post started a worldwide trend.

Fahlman posted his message on September 19, 1982. He did not keep a copy of the original, as it seemed hardly a remarkable event at the time. However, as the smiley face became more and more widespread, he realized that the original post might be of interest. It was buried deep in the Carnegie Mellon archives and not easily retrieved. Several unsuccessful attempts at looking for the old post were made over the years. In February 2002, Mike Jones of Microsoft organized an electronic equivalent of an archaeological dig through the old Carnegie Mellon backup tapes. Because the tapes were in an old format that was no longer supported, they needed special equipment to decode and play them. After searching through three years' worth of tapes (from 1981 to 1983), Jeff Baird of the Carnegie Mellon facilities staff finally found the relevant message. It read:

001101010010100111010110101010101011001010000 1

(continued from page 146)

e-mail message is sent, the user is asked to complete five simple math problems. It is hoped that a user who is not able to complete the problems will think twice and wait until morning to send the e-mail.

The Undo Send and Mail Goggles features were designed to handle some of the common problems that many users experience when using e-mail. If they become popular among Gmail users, they may find their way into other popular e-mail systems. No one, however, should rely entirely on automated tools to

01001110100101010100110010111011010100101001

"19-Sep-82 11:44 Scott E Fahlman :-)
From: Scott E Fahlman <Fahlman at Cmu-20c>

I propose that the following character sequence for joke markers:

:-)

Read it sideways. Actually, it is probably more economical to mark things that are NOT jokes, given current trends. For this, use

:-("

Fahlman remembers writing a longer message or e-mail that explained the need for joke markers in more detail, but this message was not found during the search. The smiley usage itself came under criticism; after all, if one writes clearly, it should be obvious to the audience that the tone of the writing is humorous or sarcastic. Fahlman believed that although this is true for books and other similarly distributed media, it is not the best approach for newsgroups or e-mail. In case of a book, if one reader out of many misunderstands the nature of a statement, that reader cannot do much about it because the printed medium is not accessible to the general public. On the other hand, an e-mail recipient or a newsgroup reader who missed a joke can flood the newsgroup or send out e-mails that can be misunderstood yet again by others or spark a heated discussion, which can in turn create more posts and e-mails.

It is possible that Fahlman was not the very first person to use a smiley face. In April of 1979, Kevin McKenzie used "-)" to indicate that his statement was meant as tongue-in-cheek. However, his proposition did not catch on. Fahlman's is the first documented use of a smiley that we know of and can reliably trace.

01001110100101010100110010111011010100101001

maintain proper netiquette for them. Instead, everyone should apply good common sense to their own actions on the Internet to avoid hurting, annoying, and wasting the time of others.

CONCLUSIONS

As this volume illustrates, ethical questions can be extremely difficult to resolve. In many cases, it is not possible to reach agreement about whether a particular course of action is ethical. This is one reason why people have developed rules of etiquette. If the ethical course of action in a particular situation is unclear and if there is a risk that one might unintentionally act in a way that causes someone else harm, then if everyone can at least agree on certain rules of behavior such unintentional harm can be avoided. What is important about rules of etiquette is not necessarily that they are correct in any sense, but rather that everyone agrees about what the rules are. In this way, rules of etiquette are like rules of the road; what is important is not whether the rules require one to drive on the right side or the left side of the road, only that everyone agree on which side is the correct side in order to avoid accidents.

The risk of unintentionally causing pain, annoyance, frustration, and other harms is particularly high on the Internet for a variety of reasons. First, modes of communication on the Internet, such as e-mail, text messages, and social networking sites, are widely varied and relatively new. Therefore, people have not yet had time to learn from experience about the effects of different ways of communicating. Second, the high prevalence of text-based communication on the Internet means that personal cues about the meaning of communications often are lacking. Third, messages intended for one person can be viewed by many people and vice versa. Fourth, messages intended to be read in one context (such as in an e-mail message, immediately after being written) can be read in a very different context (such as on a Web page, months after being written). For these and other reasons, there is a particularly strong need for netiquette. Anyone who has ever unintentionally been embarrassed by an e-mail message that they sent or received, only to wonder how they did not realize in advance that the problem could easily have been avoided, would do well to study the rules of netiquette that have been developed by Internet users over the years. Just a little bit of planning and forethought can often enable one to avoid many of the problems caused unintentionally by online communications.

CHRONOLOGY

1765 British government passes the first Quartering Act, requiring American colonists to provide housing to British soldiers

1776 The U.S. Declaration of Independence is approved by the Second Continental Congress

1787 Alexander Hamilton, James Madison, and John Jay publish *The Federalist* anonymously under the pseudonym Publius; these essays are now known as *The Federalist Papers*

1791 The Fourth Amendment to the U.S. Constitution is enacted as part of the Bill of Rights, providing certain protections against invasion of privacy by the U.S. government

1843 Ada Byron's notes on Charles Babbage's article are published, including a plan for calculation of Bernoulli numbers that is now recognized as the first computer program

1890 Samuel Warren and Louis Brandeis publish "The Right to Privacy," advocating a broad legal right to privacy

1958 William Higinbotham creates "Tennis for Two," a 2-D video game, at Brookhaven Lab

1968 Ivan Sutherland creates the first virtual reality device

1972 Whistle-blower W. Mark Felt (aka Deep Throat) anonymously leaks information about U.S. president Richard Nixon to journalists Bob Woodward and Carl Bernstein

1978 Multi-User Domain (MUD), the first online virtual world, is released

1979 Ray Tomlinson sends the world's first e-mail

1982	Scott Fahlman proposes use of the smiley emoticon :-)
	Philips makes the first compact disc (CD) in Germany
1985	James Moor publishes a seminal article on computer ethics entitled "What Is Computer Ethics?"
1986	U.S. Congress enacts the Electronic Communications Privacy Act (ECPA), protecting the privacy of electronic communications
1988	Robert Tappan Morris releases the Internet worm, the first computer virus to spread over the Internet
1989	German Fraunhofer Institute receives a patent for MP3 technology
1992	Association for Computing Machinery adopts Code of Ethics and Professional Conduct
1995	Phishing schemes spread on America Online (AOL) in attempts to obtain credit card numbers of AOL members
	Sally Hambridge writes "Netiquette Guidelines" (RFC 1855)
1996	U.S. Congress enacts the Health Insurance Portability and Accountability Act (HIPAA) to protect the privacy of medical records
1998	U.S. Congress enacts the Children's Online Privacy Protection Act (COPPA) to protect the privacy of minors online
1999	Melissa computer virus infects more than 1 million computers, causing $80 million in damage
	Jon Johansen releases DeCSS software code for cracking the encryption scheme on DVDs
	Shawn Fanning releases Napster
2001	First known direct phishing attack against an online payment system is launched

Napster file-sharing service is shut down by court order for copyright infringement

2002   Accounting firm Arthur Andersen convicted of obstruction of justice for shredding documents related to Enron

Cynthia Cooper and Sherron Watkins named as People of the Year by *Time* magazine for blowing the whistle on Worldcom and Enron

U.S. Supreme Court strikes down two provisions of the Child Pornography Prevention Act of 1996 for abridging freedom of speech

British computer hacker Gary McKinnon is accused by the U.S. government of hacking into 97 military and NASA computers, from which he is accused of deleting files and copying secure data; McKinnon denies the charges and claims he only searched unsecured machines for information about UFO investigations

2003   Blaster computer worm infects 500,000 computers

Second Life virtual world is launched

2004   Theft of computers from Intuit Corporation comprises security of credit cards of 47,000 customers

2006   Computer worm takes over pages on Myspace and alters links to send users to phishing Web sites intended to steal their login information

13-year-old Megan Meier commits suicide after being the victim of cyberbullying on the social networking Web site Myspace; a subsequent FBI investigation reveals that the bullying was done by the mother of an acquaintance who posed as a teenage boy

Gruesome accident scene photos of 18-year-old Nikki Catsouras, who died in a single car automobile accident, are posted on the Internet by two California Highway

Patrol officers; members of her family are haunted by the images for several years and eventually battle the CHP in court

2007   Hackers access Google "Adwords" system and steal users' passwords

Security breach at TJX comprises the security of 40 million credit card numbers

Hackers break into computer systems of Oak Ridge National Laboratory and Los Alamos National Laboratory, two of the most important labs in the United States, and gain access to personal data belonging to visitors of the lab

IBM releases guidelines to govern conduct of employees in Second Life

Facebook launches Beacon, a component of its advertising system that allows external retail Web sites to send purchase information to consumers' Facebook pages; the stated purpose of Beacon is to allow Facebook users to share their shopping activities with friends

Linden Labs bans inworld gambling in Second Life to avoid possible legal issues related to Internet gambling

Following an investigation by German police into simulated child pornography in Second Life, Linden Labs bans the depiction of sexual conduct with avatars that resemble children

Gregory Kopiloff of Seattle is arrested for attempting to use the LimeWire file-sharing system to commit identity theft; the U.S. Department of Justice reports it as the first time someone has attempted to use a file-sharing system to fraudulently access personal data

2008   Facebook simplifies privacy controls and makes default settings more permissive

The largest U.S. military base in Afghanistan is hit by an aggressive computer virus suspected to have originated in China

The Conficker computer worm is first detected; by 2010, more than 7 million computers in 200 countries are believed to be under its control

After acquiring the Napster brand and logos in bankruptcy auction and rebranding its Pressplay music service, Roxio sells Napster 2.0 to electronics retailer Best Buy for $121 million

2009   Google Dashboard is launched in response to concern about personal information gathered by the Google's applications and services; the Dashboard allows individuals to view and manage all personal data associated with their Google account

Facebook shuts down its controversial Beacon service as part of a $9.5 million settlement of a class action lawsuit

Two MIT students working on a project for an ethics and law class demonstrate that a Facebook user's network of friends can be used to determine probable sexual orientation; their "gaydar" software program raises further questions about privacy on Facebook

Three men indicted in New Jersey for the largest corporate identity theft in history; the case involves corporate data breaches that led to the theft of 130 million credit and debit card numbers

Senior U.S. Department of Defense officials report that confidential military files were compromised by unknown computer hackers over a period of two years; the stolen data included top-secret plans for the F-36 Joint Strike Fighter jet

Two of the most popular Web browsers (Internet Explorer 8 and Mozilla Firefox 3.5) introduce a privacy mode that is designed to prevent users of the same computer from knowing each other's browser history; a similar feature was introduced in Google Chrome 1.0 in late 2008

2010

Google faces investigation by government regulators and private lawyers after gathering sensitive data through unsecured Wi-Fi hot spots while collecting Google Street View images

Facebook introduces revised privacy controls that make it more difficult to change the default settings and limit access to personal information; following an outcry from users, Facebook reacts by simplifying the mechanism

Massachusetts enacts data security breach law that requires businesses that handle personal information to implement an information security program to protect personal data and prevent identity theft

In reaction to the suicides of two teenagers who were the victims of school bullies, Massachusetts legislature enacts a state law requiring school administrators to investigate reported cases of bullying; one of the teens who committed suicide was harassed by cell phone calls, text messages, and postings on social media Web sites such as Facebook

In a lawsuit brought by the Recording Industry Association of America (RIAA), federal Judge Kimba Wood rules that LimeWire, the largest peer-to-peer file-sharing service, is guilty of copyright infringement; the case is the first action against the illegal sharing of copyrighted material through file-sharing software since 2005, when a similar ruling forced Grokster to shut down

Following an interview with White House UPI bureau chief Helen Thomas, Rabbi David Nesenoff posts her negative comments about Israel's occupation of Palestine on his blog RabbiLive.com; Helen Thomas retires four days later, ending a 57-year career

In response to user demand, Facebook introduces an easy-to-locate button that allows a user to delete an account and all associated data; previously it was only possible to hide user data through deactivation

The Transportation Security Administration (TSA) rolls out body-scanning machines in airports in Oakland, California, and Spokane, Washington, despite controversy over what many see as an invasion of privacy

2011   Facebook allows application developers to access user identification details, such as names, addresses, and phone numbers

Researchers discover that iPhones and iPads constantly track the location data of the phone and save this information to a file on the user's computer

Politicians push for the Do Not Track Online Act of 2011, intended to limit the sharing and storing of consumer information by online retailers and advertisers

Large-scale data breach of the Sony Playstation Network results in the compromise of millions of user identities and credit cards

District Court Judge Harold Baker denies the request of a copyright holder to subpoena Internet Service Providers of alleged copyright infringers, holding that an IP address does not equal a person and that a warrant can only be issued for a person

Microsoft study finds that schools are ill prepared to teach students the basics of online safety, security, and ethics

GLOSSARY

anonymity   communicating without revealing your true identity, such as by publishing an article without your name on it

anonymized data   data from which personally identifying information has been removed; an example would be a record of a hospital patient in which the patient's name and Social Security number have been deleted

anonymous remailer   a service that strips your name and e-mail address from e-mail that you send and then forwards the e-mail to the recipient so that your identity remains hidden

antivirus software   a type of software used to protect a computer from infection by viruses and other malware

Association for Computing Machinery [ACM]   a professional association of computer scientists that has created the ACM Code of Ethics and Professional Conduct

attribution   credit given to an author when that author's work is cited in another work; attribution is provided to acknowledge the work of the other author and to avoid charges of plagiarism

avatar   a graphical representation of a computer user, usually an animated character representing the user in a video game or other VIRTUAL WORLD

back door   a bug intentionally placed into software by a programmer to enable the programmer to break into the software at a later date

bug   an error or failure in computer software that results in a system crash, incorrect data, or some other unexpected result; most bugs are caused by errors in the logic implemented by the software programmer

CAPTCHA   an acronym for Completely Automated Public Turing test to tell Computers and Humans Apart; CAPTCHAs often are used to prevent software from logging into Web sites to engage in identity theft and other nefarious activities

caveat   a known software bug, disclosed by the software's vendor upon releasing the software

closed circuit television (CCTV) camera   a frequently used type of SURVEILLANCE CAMERA

cloud computing   storing data and executing software on a network, such as the Internet, so that such data and programs can be accessed from a remote location instead of being stored and executed on a user's local computer

code of ethics   a set of ethical rules or guidelines, usually written by a professional organization, describing actions that are considered ethical in a particular profession

code review   the process of reviewing the source code of a computer program in an effort to uncover security flaws and other bugs; code review often is performed before releasing safety-critical software to the public

computer ethics   a branch of philosophy that deals with standards of conduct related to computers and how computer professionals should make responsible decisions

computer network   a collection of interconnected computers capable of communicating with each other over their connections

computer security   a field that attempts to protect computers, networks, and data from attacks

confidential information   refers to information that is only intended to be seen by certain people and be kept hidden from others

cookies   data used by Web sites to record information about Web site visitors

cyberbullying   online bullying of one young person by another

cyberharassment   online harassment of one adult by another

cyberstalking   tracking and following another person using the Internet, often involving repeatedly sending the person unwanted messages despite the person's instructions to stop

data integrity the extent to which data remains unchanged over time so that its contents may be relied upon to be accurate; data integrity is one aspect of COMPUTER SECURITY

data security the extent to which computer data are protected against access by parties who are not authorized to make such access

deadlock a software bug caused by multiple software components, each of which is waiting for the other to complete, thereby causing the software to cease functioning

Deep Throat one of the most famous INTERNAL WHISTLE-BLOWERS in U.S. history, who revealed information about U.S. president Richard Nixon's unlawful activities to journalists; his identity was revealed more than 30 years after his whistle-blowing activities

de-identified data See ANONYMIZED DATA

document retention policy a policy, typically adopted by a company or government agency, that includes rules specifying how long different types of documents are to be retained before they are destroyed

e-mail attachment a file, such as music or software, that is attached to an e-mail message, that can be used to transmit computer VIRUSES

emoticon a combination of characters, usually inserted into an e-mail message, that looks like a human face expressing an emotion, such as :-)

employer privacy policy a policy created by a company or other employer that explains whether the employer will treat its employees' e-mails and other information as private

etiquette rules of behavior designed to avoid embarrassment, offense, and insult in human interactions

external whistle-blower a WHISTLE-BLOWER who works outside an organization and exposes information about that organization to the public; external whistle-blowers often are journalists

fair use the use of a copyrighted work for purposes such as education or research, such that the use of the copyrighted work does not constitute copyright INFRINGEMENT

file-sharing software   a type of software that enables people to copy and transmit files, such as songs and movies, among each other over the Internet without having to manually send the files

flaming   engaging in extremely heated debates on the Internet long after other participants have expressed their desire for the debate to end

Freedom of Information Act (FOIA)   a U.S. federal law that requires that the government provide information about government activities to members of the public upon request; FOIA is an example of a SUNSHINE LAW

glitch   a minor software bug; sometimes refers to bugs in video games that cause the game to exhibit strange behavior, such as the ability of characters to walk through walls, but do not cause the game to crash

graphics accelerator card   a component of a computer, often purchasable and installable separately, for generating graphics more quickly than the computer's main processor

griefer   someone who intentionally engages in activity in a VIRTUAL WORLD for the purpose of attacking, annoying, or offending other RESIDENTS

griefing   the activity in which GRIEFERS engage

harassment   physical actions or statements that threaten or intimidate someone else; most Internet service providers and Web sites have policies that prohibit harassment on their systems

identity theft   using someone else's e-mail address, social security number, or other personally identifying information to impersonate that person

infringement   copying a Web site, song, video, or other copyrighted work without permission from the copyright owner and without a justification that qualifies as FAIR USE

internal whistle-blower   a WHISTLE-BLOWER who works in an organization and exposes information about that organization's unlawful or unethical activities to the public

Internet Protocol (IP)   the method by which data moves from computer to computer on the Internet

inworld   an adjective that applies to activities performed within a VIRTUAL WORLD; for example, someone who buys a house in a virtual world is said to buy the house inworld

key logger   software that monitors and records the keystrokes of a computer user, typically without the user's knowledge

local area network (LAN)   a COMPUTER NETWORK connecting computers within a limited area, such as a home, business, or school

malware   harmful software, such as VIRUSES and SPYWARE

metaverse   a combination of multiple VIRTUAL WORLDS

MOO (MUD object oriented)   an online virtual reality system that is text-based and allows multiple users (or players) to be connected at the same time; object oriented indicates that players can use object oriented programming to modify the system's database of objects

multi-user domain (MUD)   an early kind of VIRTUAL WORLD in which multiple users can interact online, usually as players in a game

netiquette   guidelines for behaving online in a way that is respectful to others; online ETIQUETTE

password protection   a method of limiting access to software or a Web site by assigning each user a secret password that must be provided to gain access to the software or Web site

payload   the portion of a computer virus that performs the function for which the virus was designed, such as copying or destroying data

phishing   tricking a user into visiting a fake Web site, such as a fake version of a bank's Web site, to entice the user to enter his or her username and password for the purpose of IDENTITY THEFT

pirating   a term used by copyright owners to refer to copying music, videos, and other copyrighted works without the copyright owner's permission

plagiarism   copying text from someone else's work into your own work, without providing a footnote or other citation to the original work

privacy   the concept that every person is entitled to a sphere, such as his or her own home, that is free from intrusion by the government or anyone else

proxy server   a server that acts as an intermediary between a source and destination in a computer network; some proxy servers are used to enable users to engage in anonymous communication

public domain   novels, poems, plays, music, artwork, and other creative works that are not protected by copyright and therefore may be used freely by anyone without first obtaining the permission of the work's creator

Publius   a pseudonym used by the authors of the Federalist Papers, a series of 85 essays that argued for ratification of the U.S. Constitution; the authors were Alexander Hamilton, James Madison, and John Jay

reasonable expectation of privacy   the kind and degree of privacy that it is reasonable to expect in a given set of circumstances; often used by the legal system to determine whether the law should protect a person's privacy in a particular situation

resident   someone who inhabits a virtual world through an AVATAR

responsible disclosure   the process of informing a software company of bugs that you discover in the company's software before you reveal those bugs to the public

sampling   copying a small portion of someone else's song or video into your own song or video

sarcasm   a kind of humor in which a statement is intended to mean the opposite of what it says, which is easily misinterpreted in e-mails and other online communication

Second Life   a virtual world accessible on the Internet, developed by Linden Lab and launched in 2003

security   protecting a building, person, computer, network, software, or other object from attack

server farm   a large collection of computer servers, typically used by Internet search engines, virtual worlds, and other online services that require massive amounts of computing power to provide services over the Internet to their users

slander   making a false statement about another person in a way that harms the person's reputation

smiley an iconic representation of a smiling face (also called happy face) that usually consists of a yellow circle, two black dots for eyes, and a black arc for a mouth; often used as a general term to refer to any emoticon

spam e-mail sent to people who did not request it; spam is usually sent in the millions to advertise products and services or to promote scams

spyware software that secretly monitors actions performed by a computer's users, such as tracking the products a user purchases in order to send advertisements to the user for similar products

sunshine law a law that entitles members of the public to attend government meetings and/or obtain records of public proceedings; the Freedom of Information Act is an example of a sunshine law

surveillance camera a camera used to monitor the location and actions of people, typically without the knowledge of the people being monitored

typosquatting purchasing a domain name that is similar to a domain name owned by someone else, usually differing only in a minor change in spelling, in an attempt to ensnare Web users who accidentally mistype a domain name

URL hijacking See TYPOSQUATTING

video card See GRAPHICS ACCELERATOR CARD

virtual child pornography pornography that appears to depict real children but does not

virtual property real estate and resources that exist only in a VIRTUAL WORLD created by computer software

virtual world a simulated world, which exists only inside computer software, in which people interact with each other using AVATARS

virus software that installs itself on someone's computer to perform a harmful action, such as destroying data on the computer or copying financial information

Web-monitoring software software that monitors and records the Web sites visited by a user and other actions taken by the user on the Web, typically without the knowledge of the user

whistle-blower   a person who reveals confidential information about the government or a company in order to expose wrongdoing

white hat hacker   a hacker who engages in hacking for beneficial purposes, such as revealing security flaws in software

WikiLeaks   an international nonprofit media organization that publishes private, classified, or secret information from various sources

workaround   an action that a user of software can perform to avoid the negative consequences of a bug in the software

FURTHER RESOURCES

The following resources are arranged according to chapter title.

"Privacy: Does It Exist Online?"

BOOKS

Caloyannides, Michael A. *Privacy Protection and Computer Forensics.* Boston, Mass.: Artech House Publishers, 2004. A comprehensive how-to manual for protecting private data stored on computers and electronic devices such as cell phones, GPS units, and PDAs. Explains where sensitive data is stored on these devices and how to remove it. This book also covers the most common threats to online privacy and the best ways to avoid them.

Hawke, Constance S. *Computer and Internet Use on Campus: A Legal Guide to Issues of Intellectual Property, Free Speech, and Privacy.* San Francisco, Calif.: Jossey-Bass, 2000. An overview of the legal and ethical issues surrounding technology and Internet use on college and university campuses. Includes examples, recommendations, and guidelines for educators and academic administrators.

Howard, Rick. *Cyber Fraud: Tactics, Techniques and Procedures.* Boca Raton, Fla.: Auerbach, 2009. This in-depth study of the culture of cyber crime combines investigative reporting with technical analysis. Uses a variety of illustrations and case studies to explore cyber threats and the cyber fraud underground, as well as the technical innovations that have evolved as a result.

Johnson, Deborah G. *Computer Ethics.* Upper Saddle River, N.J.: Prentice Hall, 2009. The fourth edition of this seminal work combines law, philosophy, and technology in an examination of the ethical use of computers. A separate chapter is devoted to privacy and the role of computers in collecting and distributing personal information.

McLean, Bethany. *The Smartest Guys in the Room: The Amazing Rise and Scandalous Fall of Enron.* New York: Portfolio Trade, 2004. A chronicle of the rise and fall of Enron, the Texas-based energy corporation that engaged in financial deception and corporate-wide accounting fraud, leading to a spectacular bankruptcy in 2001. This book focuses on the lack of accountability and professional ethics in the Enron corporate culture.

Solove, Daniel. *The Digital Person: Technology and Privacy in the Information Age.* New York: NYU Press, 2006. An analysis of the current state of privacy in the information age. Solove, an associate law professor at George Washington University Law School, explains how privacy is being compromised by computer databases and suggests systemwide changes to restore privacy.

ARTICLES

Duffy, Michael. "By the Sign of the Crooked E." *Time,* 19 January 2002. Available online. URL: http://www.time.com/time/business/article/0,8599, 195268,00.html. Accessed January 25, 2011. An interview with Sherron Watkins, the Enron vice president who blew the whistle on the corporation's malfeasance.

Krawetz, Dr. Neal. "Online Impersonations: No Validation Required." *The Register,* 23 April 2007. Available online. URL: http://www.theregister. co.uk/2007/04/23/online_impersonations_validation. Accessed February 15, 2011. Examples of how impersonation occurs on the Internet and tips for spotting impersonators.

Martinez, Alejandro. "Simitian's Bill Aimed at Online Impersonation." *San Francisco Chronicle,* 9 August 2010. Available online. URL: http://articles. sfgate.com/2010-08-09/business/22212438_1_e-mail-stories-internet-law. Accessed February 15, 2011. Describes a recent case of e-mail impersonation and a proposed California law that will make malicious online impersonation a crime.

Microsoft Office. "Encrypt E-mail Messages." Microsoft Office Outlook 2007 Help. Available online. URL: http://office.microsoft.com/en-us/outlook-help/encrypt-e-mail-messages-HP001230536.aspx. Accessed February 15, 2011. Microsoft support information describing how to encrypt e-mail messages in Office Outlook 2007.

Wolgemuth, Liz. "5 Ways Your Computer Use Can Get You Fired." *U.S. News & World Report* Money Blog, March 11, 2008. Available online. URL:

http://money.usnews.com/money/careers/articles/2008/03/11/5-ways-your-computer-use-can-get-you-fired.html. Accessed February 15, 2011. Lists the types of computer use that are frowned on by most employers.

Zetter, Kim. "Court: Cyberbullying Threats Are Not Protected Speech." *Wired Threat Level Blog*, March 18, 2010. Available online. URL: http://www.wired.com/threatlevel/2010/03/cyberbullying-not-protected. Accessed February 15, 2011. After a 15-year-old California boy received comments that included threats of violence and death on his Web site, his parents sought justice in criminal and then civil court. This article examines the various court rulings in the case, including a decision that online messages with harmful intent do not constitute free speech.

WEB SITES

Cyberbullying. Available online. URL: http://www.ncpc.org/cyberbullying. Accessed February 15, 2011. Information about the National Crime Prevention Council's advertising campaign targeting cyberbullying. Includes resources related to the prevention of cyberbullying.

Cyberbullying Research Center. Available online. URL: http://www.cyberbullying.us. Accessed February 15, 2011. A clearinghouse for information related to adolescents and technology, intended as a resource for parents, teachers, counselors, and others who work with youth.

i-SAFE. Available online. URL: http://isafe.org. Accessed February 15, 2011. Founded in 1998, i-SAFE is a leading provider of Internet safety education materials. According to the i-SAFE Web site, more than 21 million students have completed i-SAFE lessons.

Privacy Rights Clearinghouse. Available online. URL: http://www.privacyrights.org. Accessed February 15, 2011. Web site for a nonprofit organization that provides information about how technology affects personal privacy.

Stop Cyberbullying. Available online. URL: http://www.stopcyberbullying.org. Accessed February 15, 2011. Information about cyberbullying including advice for specific age groups from seven to 17.

Times Topics: Megan Meir. Available online. URL: http://topics.nytimes.com/topics/reference/timestopics/people/m/megan_meier/index.html. Accessed February 15, 2011. An overview of the facts surrounding the case of 13-year-old Megan Meier, who committed suicide as a result of cyberbullying committed by an adult neighbor posing as a teenage boy. Includes links to related *New York Times* articles.

Tor. Available online. URL: https://www.torproject.org/index.html.en. Accessed February 15, 2011. Provides free software and an open network system that hides a user's IP address when visiting many Web sites.

WiredSafety.org. Available online. URL: http://www.wiredsafety.org. Accessed February 15, 2011. WiredSafety is a worldwide network of volunteers who provide educational materials related to technology safety and advice to victims of cybercrime and harassment. Their Web site is a resource for parents, children, technology workers, educators, and lawmakers. Includes access to a helpline for advice on cyberbullying, cyberstalking, and cyberabuse.

"Security: Challenges in the Information Society"

BOOKS

Lehtinen, Rick, Deborah Russell, and G. T. Gangemi. *Computer Security Basics.* Sebastopol, Calif.: O'Reilly Media, 2006. The fundamentals of computer security, including an examination of viruses, malicious software, and Web attacks. Also includes information about U.S. government security standards and "Orange Book" certification.

Mitnick, Kevin D. *The Art of Intrusion: The Real Stories Behind the Exploits of Hackers, Intruders and Deceivers.* Indianapolis, Ind.: Wiley, 2005. In the early 1990s, Kevin Mitnick was the most wanted computer criminal in the United States. Following his arrest and conviction, he served a five-year prison sentence for hacking into computer systems. He now is a computer security consultant and in this book tells the stories of hackers who have breached the secure computer systems of major corporations.

Schneier, Bruce. *Schneier on Security.* Indianapolis, Ind.: Wiley, 2008. Schneier, one of the foremost experts in computer security, provides advice on computer security. Includes real-life examples of security issues related to a wide variety of computer systems. This book consists of articles previously published on Schneier's Web site and blog.

———. *Secrets and Lies: Digital Security in a Networked World.* Indianapolis, Ind.: Wiley, 2004. Schneier, an expert in cryptography and electronic security, uses humor and insight to describe the current state of threats to computer security and strategies for implementing more secure systems.

ARTICLES

Bowden, Mark. "The Enemy Within." *Atlantic,* June 2010. Available online. URL: http://www.theatlantic.com/magazine/archive/2010/06/the-enemy-within/8098/. Accessed February 15, 2011. Describes the appearance of the Conficker computer worm, the efforts to eradicate it, and its continuing threat.

Bradley, Tony. "How to Stop 11 Hidden Security Threats." *PCWorld,* January 24, 2010. Available online. URL: http://www.pcworld.com/article/187199/how_to_stop_11_hidden_security_threats.html?tk=rel_news. Accessed February 15, 2011. Describes how antivirus software and a firewall can't stop all attacks on a personal computer and provides suggestions for additional security protection.

Messmer, Ellen. "Security Flag: 'Responsible Disclosure' Debate Flares Anew." *Network World,* May 31, 2007. Available online. URL: http://www.networkworld.com/news/2007/053107-security-flap.html. Accessed February 15, 2011. Discusses the pros and cons of public hacking contests as a means of discovering hidden software vulnerabilities.

Seltzer, Larry. "'I Love You' Virus Turns Ten: What Have We Learned?" *PC Magazine Digital Edition,* April 28, 2010. Available online. URL: http://www.pcmag.com/article2/0,2817,2363172,00.asp. Accessed February 15, 2011. When the virus struck in 2000, it was the biggest malware event in history. This article looks back at the effects of the ILOVEYOU virus from the perspective of 10 years later.

Wujek, Dr. Joseph H. "Software Testing." Online Ethics Center for Engineering (February 16, 2006). Available online. URL: http://www.onlineethics.org/Resources/Cases/EE22.aspx. Accessed February 15, 2011. A case study that illustrates the ethical decisions facing developers of life-critical software.

WEB SITES

McAfee Security Advice Center. Available online. URL: http://home.mcafee.com/AdviceCenter/Default.aspx?id=ad_vp_htpycavawa. Accessed February 15, 2011. Advice from one of the leading computer security companies about how to protect a computer from viruses and worm attacks.

Microsoft Online Safety. Available online. URL: http://www.microsoft.com/ protect/default.aspx. Accessed February 15, 2011. A Microsoft resource with advice on password protection, computer security, and safe social networking.

PewInternet Trend Data. Available online. URL: http://www.pewinternet.org/ Static-Pages/Trend-Data/Online-Activites-Total.aspx. Accessed February 15, 2011. A report on who uses the Internet and typical daily online activities.

"Anonymity: Advantages and Dangers of Anonymous Communication"

BOOKS

Ackerman, Bruce A., and Ian Ayres. *Voting with Dollars: A New Paradigm for Campaign Finance.* New Haven, Conn.: Yale University Press, 2002. Examines alternative approaches to campaign finance reform. The authors are two leading law professors who challenge the existing campaign reform agenda and suggest that all contributions should be made anonymously.

Alford, C. Fred. *Whistleblowers: Broken Lives and Organizational Power.* Ithaca, N.Y.: Cornell University Press, 2002. An examination of the motivations and experiences of people who choose to confront an organization despite the possibility of alienation from coworkers, friends, and family. Alford also analyzes the ethics involved in the act of whistle-blowing.

Ellsberg, Daniel. *Secrets: A Memoir of Vietnam and the Pentagon Papers.* New York: Penguin, 2003. In 1971, Daniel Ellsberg was a Defense Department analyst who became disenchanted with U.S. foreign policy and released classified documents about the Vietnam War to the *New York Times.* This book tells the story of Ellsberg's journey from Defense Department adviser to antiwar protester and activist.

Gillmor, Dan. *We the Media: Grassroots Journalism by the People, for the People.* Sebastopol, Calif.: O'Reilly Media, 2006. Gillmor, a columnist for the *San Jose Mercury News,* is an advocate of grassroots media. He makes the case that the news no longer belongs to establishment media but is in the hands of personal bloggers, members of Internet forums, videographers, photographers, and even users of e-mail.

Rosenberg, Scott. *Say Everything: How Blogging Began, What It's Becoming, and Why It Matters.* New York: Crown, 2009. A 15-year history of blogging, including its impact on the media, business, politics, and the personal lives of bloggers. Rosenberg shows how blogging turned the Internet from a passive medium to an expressive, democratic, and collective experience.

ARTICLES

Crosbie, Vin. "Time to Get Tough: Managing Anonymous Reader Comments." OJR: The Online Journalism Review (January 26, 2006). Available online. URL: http://www.ojr.org/ojr/stories/060126crosbie. Accessed February 15, 2011. An examination of the history of pseudonymity in American opinion journalism and the problems associated with anonymous online commentaries.

Fildes, Jonathan. "What Is WikiLeaks?" BBC Mobile. (October 23, 2010) Available online. URL: http://www.bbc.co.uk/news/technology-10757263. Accessed February 15, 2011. An examination of the WikiLeaks whistle-blowing Web site.

Hart, Bryan. "The Internet's Anonymity Problem." The Faculty Blog, University of Chicago Law School (November 12, 2008). Available online. URL: http://uchicagolaw.typepad.com/faculty/2008/11/chicagos-best-i.html. Accessed February 15, 2011. Comments on a lecture on the legal aspects of defamation on the Internet given by Dean Saul Levmore of the University of Chicago Law School.

Hoyt, Clark. "Those Persistent Anonymous Sources." *New York Times,* March 21, 2009. Available online. URL: http://www.nytimes.com/2009/03/22/opinion/22pubed.html?_r=1. Accessed February 15, 2011. A former editor at *The New York Times* describes the newspaper's policy on anonymous sources and gives examples of situations where an anonymous source was used. The pros and cons of anonymous sources are also discussed.

Smith, Terence. "Lurking in the Shadows." *The News Hour with Jim Lehrer,* September 30, 1998. Available online. URL: http://www.pbs.org/newshour/bb/media/july-dec98/sources_9-30.html. Accessed February 15, 2011. Transcript of a radio program featuring correspondent Terrence Smith leading a discussion about the use of anonymous sources with two journalists and a White House official who has acted as an anonymous source.

WEB SITES

Times Topics: Jeffrey Wigand. Available online. URL: http://topics.nytimes.com/topics/reference/timestopics/people/w/jeffrey_wigand/index.html.

Accessed February 15, 2011. Archive of *New York Times* articles about Jeffery Wigand, the former vice president at Brown & Williamson Tobacco who became nationally known as a whistle-blower when he disclosed company secrets about the nicotine content in his company's tobacco.

WikiLeaks.org. Available online. URL: http://wikileaks.org. Accessed February 15, 2011. Online depository for classified documents, videos, and images.

"Virtual Worlds: Living inside Your Computer"

BOOKS

Bartle, Richard. *Designing Virtual Worlds.* Indianapolis, Ind.: New Riders Games, 2003. A definitive treatment on the design of computer virtual worlds, describing in detail the process of virtual world development. Includes information about the history of virtual worlds and theories about their appeal. Bartle is a pioneer and design consultant in the field of virtual worlds.

Castronova, Edward. *Synthetic Worlds: The Business and Culture of Online Games.* Chicago, Ill.: University of Chicago Press, 2006. A comprehensive look at the impact of online gaming on business and culture. Castronova makes the case that many Internet-based multiplayer games have become virtual societies with working economic systems and a community experience that for many players is more attractive than the real world.

Guest, Tim. *Second Lives: A Journey Through Virtual Worlds.* New York: Random House, 2008. A look at the world of online virtual reality, from Second Life to EverQuest, and the people that spend time there. Examines the benefits that many people have found in virtual worlds, as well as the dark side of this alternative reality.

Meadows, Mark Stephen. *I, Avatar: The Culture and Consequences of Having a Second Life.* Berkeley, Calif.: New Riders Press, 2008. An illustrated history of online avatars as well as an exploration of the role they play in online interactions. This is also a personal account of the author's experiences in the virtual world of Second Life.

White, Brian A. *Second Life: A Guide to Your Virtual World.* Indianapolis, Ind.: Que, 2007. A far-reaching guide to the virtual world of Second Life. Includes step-by-step tutorials as well as interviews with dozens of Second Life residents. Both novice and veterans users will find information in this guide that will enhance their experience of Second Life.

ARTICLES

Becker, David. "Inflicting pain on 'griefers.'" CNET News, December 13, 2004. Available online. URL: http://news.cnet.com/Inflicting-pain-on-griefers/ 2100-1043_3-5488403.html. Accessed February 15, 2011. Describes how game companies are using technology, psychology, and sociology to fight the damage inflicted by griefers.

Brenner, Susan W. "Is There Such a Thing as 'Virtual Crime'?" *California Criminal Law Review,* University of California, Berkeley, 2001. Available online. URL: http://www.boalt.org/CCLR/v4/v4brenner.htm. Accessed February 15, 2011. Discusses the legal definition of cybercrime and compares and contrasts it with crime in the real world.

Dibbell, Julian. "A Rape in Cyberspace." Julian Dibbell Web site, 1998. Available online. URL: http://www.juliandibbell.com/articles/a-rape-in-cyberspace. Accessed February 15, 2011. Chapter One of Dibbell's book *My Tiny Life,* describing the controversial "virtual rape" that took place in the LambdaMOO online virtual community.

Erler, Alexander. "Should We Be Afraid of Virtual Reality?" University of Oxford Practical Ethics Web site, 28 September 2009. Available online. URL: http://www.practicalethicsnews.com/practicalethics/2009/09/ should-we-be-afraid-of-virtual-reality.html. Accessed February 15, 2011. Examines some of the common concerns about the popularity of virtual worlds, including social disaffiliation and a loss of authenticity in real life.

Hof, Robert D. "My Virtual Life." *Bloomberg Businessweek,* May 1, 2006. Available online. URL: http://www.businessweek.com/magazine/content/06_18/b3982001.htm. Accessed February 15, 2011. An exploration of the economy of Second Life, including property rights, the production of virtual goods and the exchange of goods and services.

WEB SITES

State of Play. *New York Law School Review* 49, no. 1 (2004). Available online. URL: http://www.nyls.edu/academics/jd_programs/law_review/published_ issues/state_of_play_volume_49_no_1. Accessed February 15, 2011. Web site with links to articles covering a variety of legal and ethical topics related to virtual worlds.

Virtual Worlds Timeline. Available online. URL: http://www.vwtimeline. com. Accessed February 15, 2011. Official Web site for the Virtual Worlds

Timeline project. The goal of the project is to track the origins and evolution of social virtual worlds that center on communication and interaction rather than game playing.

"Professional Ethics: When Is the Programmer Responsible?"

BOOKS

Bynum, Terrell Ward, and Simon Rogerson. *Computer Ethics and Professional Responsibility.* Malden, Mass.: Wiley-Blackwell, 2003. A collection of significant papers from key experts in the field of computer ethics. Topics include the history of computer ethics, professional codes of ethics, computer crime, computer security, and the debate over intellectual property rights and the open source movement.

Ford, Daniel F. *Three Mile Island: Thirty Minutes to Meltdown.* New York: Penguin, 1982. A detailed examination of the 1979 events that led to a near-meltdown at the Metropolitan Edison nuclear power station in Pennsylvania. Ford analyzes the human errors and regulatory failures that caused the incident that came to be known as the Three Mile Island accident.

Neumann, Peter G. *Computer Related Risks.* Reading, Mass.: Addison-Wesley Professional, 1994. A study of computer problems caused by software, hardware, human error, and natural disasters. Causes, effects, and strategies for avoidance are discussed. This book is based on data compiled by the ACM (Association for Computing Machinery) International Risks Forum.

Peterson, Ivars. *Fatal Defect: Chasing Killer Computer Bugs.* New York: Vintage, 1996. As exciting as a crime novel, this book describes serious computer bugs and the computer detectives who hunt them down. It also discusses how software engineers use the information they derive from investigating bugs to design processes that help prevent the errors from recurring.

ARTICLES

Boehm, Barry, and Victor R. Basili. "Software Defect Reduction Top 10 List." University of Maryland Publications, January 2001. Available online. URL: http://www.cs.umd.edu/projects/SoftEng/ESEG/papers/82.78.pdf. Accessed February 15, 2011. Discussed causes of software defects and provides 10 techniques for reducing the occurrence of defects.

Cosgrove-Mather, Bootie. "Software Bugs Can Be Lethal." CBS News (April 29, 2003). Available online. URL: http://www.cbsnews.com/stories/2003/04/29/tech/main551492.shtml. Accessed February 15, 2011. Discusses the growing impact of software bugs due to computer chips embedded in everything from gadgets to household appliances to critical systems like power plants. Includes an interview with software defect expert Peter Neumann.

Garfinkel, Simson. "History's Worst Software Bugs." *Wired,* November 8, 2005. Available online. URL: http://www.wired.com/software/coolapps/news/2005/11/69355. Accessed February 15, 2011. *Wired*'s chronological list of the top 10 worst software bugs of all time.

WEB SITES

ACM Code of Ethics and Professional Conduct. Association for Computing Machinery. Available online. URL: http://www.acm.org/about/code-of-ethics. Accessed February 15, 2011. Statements of personal responsibility adopted by a professional association for computing professionals.

Computer Ethics Institute. Available online. URL: http://www.computerethicsinstitute.com. Accessed February 15, 2011. Web site for nonprofit organization that focuses on the ethics of computer technology. Founded by Dr. Ramon C. Barquin, author of seminal 1992 paper entitled "In Pursuit of 'Ten Commandments' for Computer Ethics."

IEEE Code of Ethics. Institute of Electrical and Electronics Engineers. Available online. URL: http://www.ieee.org/membership_services/membership/ethics_code.html. Accessed February 15, 2011. Code of conduct adopted by association for electronics professionals.

Peter G. Neumann. SRI International Computer Science Laboratory. Available online. URL: http://www.csl.sri.com/users/neumann. Accessed February 15, 2011. Home page for software defects expert Peter Neumann; includes links to research works related to software defects.

"Copying: Does Ease of Copying Make It Right?"

BOOKS

Alderman, John. *Sonic Boom: Napster, P2P and the Battle for the Future of Music.* Cambridge, Mass.: Perseus Publishing, 2001. The first full-length examination of online music trading, this book describes the power struggles between the established music industry and MP3 file swapping Web sites like Napster. Author Alderman, a journalist who was written for *Wired,* covers the technical, historical, legal, and ethical aspects of the Napster case.

Gilmore, Barry. *Plagiarism: Why It Happens and How to Prevent It.* Portsmouth, Mass.: Heinemann, 2008. A guide for preventing academic plagiarism and dealing with it when it occurs. This book presents research and writing suggestions to help students recognize and avoid plagiarism.

Mallon, Thomas. *Stolen Words—The Classic Book on Plagiarism.* Orlando, Fla.: Harvest Books 2001. A scholarly look at the unattributed use of the writing of others, including some famous examples. The author is a literary detective who delves into the motivation of plagiarizers and the consequences of their actions. Also covers plagiarism in academia, the entertainment industry, and politics.

Mnookin, Seth. *Hard News: Twenty-one Brutal Months at the* New York Times *and How They Changed the American Media.* New York: Random House Trade Paperbacks, 2005. This book reads like a thriller in its description of how a young *New York Times* reporter named Jayson Blair was able to publish articles that were both plagiarized and fabricated, and how he was discovered. This book also describes the devastating effect of Blair's actions on the reputation of the *New York Times.*

Vicinus, Martha, and Caroline Eisner, eds. *Originality, Imitation, and Plagiarism: Teaching Writing in the Digital Age.* Ann Arbor: University of Michigan Press, 2008. A collection of essays that explores how the Internet affects original writing. Issues touched on include ownership of original work and copyright conventions.

ARTICLES

McManus, Sean. "A Short History of File Sharing" (August 2003). Available online. URL: http://www.sean.co.uk/a/musicjournalism/var/historyoffile sharing.shtm. Accessed February 15, 2011. A history of Napster and the legal issues that led to its demise as a file sharing application.

WEB SITES

Copyright and Fair Use in the Classroom, on the Internet, and the World Wide Web. University of Maryland Information and Library Science. Available online. URL: http://www.umuc.edu/library/copy.shtml. Accessed February

15, 2011. An introduction to copyright and fair use policy designed to help students and faculty make informed decisions about using materials from the Internet.

Copyright on the Internet. University of New Hampshire School of Law. Available online. URL: http://law.unh.edu/thomasfield/ipbasics/copyright-on-the-internet.php. Accessed February 15, 2011. Discussion of legal issues centering around copyrights and fair use on the Internet.

RIAA v. The People: Five Years Later. Electronic Frontier Foundation. (September, 2008). Available online. URL: http://www.eff.org/wp/riaa-v-people-years-later. Accessed February 15, 2011. A history of the legal actions taken by the Recording Industry Association of America (RIAA) against users of peer-to-peer file sharing software.

"Speech: The Internet as Library, Newspaper, Television, and Beyond"

BOOKS

Atkins, Robert, and Svetlana Mintcheva, eds. *Censoring Culture: Contemporary Threats to Free Expression.* New York: The New Press, 2006. A collection of essays representing thoughts on censorship from contemporary experts in media, the arts, law, technology, psychology, and education.

Deibert, Ronald J., John G. Palfrey, Rafal Rohozinski, and Jonathan Zittrain, eds. *Access Denied: The Practice and Policy of Global Internet Filtering.* Cambridge, Mass.: MIT Press, 2008. This book documents and analyzes Internet filtering and censorship in countries around the world. Information from a survey completed by the OpenNet Initiative is used as a basis for an examination of the social, legal, and political implications of filtering.

Godwin, Mike. *Cyber Rights: Defending Free Speech in the Digital Age.* Cambridge, Mass.: MIT Press, 2003. Godwin, a counsel to the Electronic Frontier Foundation, examines a variety of Internet First Amendment cases and issues. This book reflects the author's position as an activist for civil liberties in cyberspace.

Hawke, Constance S. *Computer and Internet Use on Campus: A Legal Guide to Issues of Intellectual Property, Free Speech, and Privacy.* San Francisco, Calif.: Jossey-Bass, 2000. A resource book intended to inform educators and campus administrators about legal and ethical issues surrounding the use of computers and the Internet on campus. Includes case studies, recommendations, and guidelines for university officials.

Silverman, David S. *You Can't Air That: Four Cases of Controversy and Censorship in American Television Programming.* Syracuse, N.Y.: Syracuse University Press, 2007. An analysis of four controversial television programs and the use of network censorship, intimidation by sponsors, and broadcasting regulation to manipulate artistic expression and freedom of speech.

ARTICLES

Kessler, Ryder. "Obscenity, Censorship, and the First Amendment." *Atlantic.* Available online. URL: http://www.theatlantic.com/magazine/archive/2006/07/obscenity-censorship-and-the-first-amendment/5073. Accessed February 15, 2011. A summary of *Atlantic* writings from the past 100 years covering the First Amendment, obscenity and freedom of speech.

Levine, Robert. "Unlocking the iPod." *Fortune,* 23 October 2006. Available online. URL: http://money.cnn.com/magazines/fortune/fortune_archive/2006/10/30/8391726/index.htm. Accessed February 15, 2011. Describes the exploits of prodigy hacker Jon Johansen, who at age 15 helped author a program that removed DVD encryption and at 22 reversed engineered Apple's FairPlay encryption technology.

WEB SITES

First Amendment in History. Illinois First Amendment Center. Available online. URL: http://www.illinoisfirstamendmentcenter.com/history.php. Accessed February 15, 2011. A history of the First Amendment, censorship, and current issues.

Reno v. ACLU. OYEZ (U.S. Supreme Court Media). Available online. URL: http://www.oyez.org/cases/1990-1999/1996/1996_96_511. Accessed February 15, 2011. A summary of the United States Supreme Court ruling in the case of *Reno v. the American Civil Liberties Union,* which struck down anti-indecency portions of the Communications Decency Act of 1996.

"Netiquette: Adding Formality to an Informal Medium"

BOOKS

Baron, Naomi S. *Always On: Language in an Online and Mobile World.* New York: Oxford University Press, 2008. A handbook for understanding electronic communication, from instant messaging to cell phones to Facebook and blogs. This books also looks at the language of the online and mobile worlds.

Chan, Janis Fisher. *E-Mail: A Write It Well Guide.* Oakland, Calif.: Write It Well, 2008. Guidelines and tips for writing professional e-mail. This book includes suggestions on how to get the best results from e-mail communication and how to avoid some of the inherent problems.

Crystal, David. *Txtng: The Gr8 Db8.* New York: Oxford University Press, 2008. An examination of text messaging and its impact on society. The author, an expert in linguistics, looks with humor and insight at the effects of texting on language and culture.

Kallos, Judith. *Because Netiquette Matters!* Bloomington, Ind.: Xlibris Corporation, 2004. This reference book uses an accessible, conversational tone to explain the ground rules for personal and business e-mail and online etiquette.

Meyer, Verne, Pat Sebranek, and John Van Rys. *Writing Effective E-Mail: Practical Strategies for Strengthening Electronic Communication.* Burlington, Wis.: Upwrite Press, 2005. A concise guide to using e-mail effectively for business. Includes warnings about some of the common e-mail pitfalls as well as language tips and exercises.

ARTICLES

Mohum, Sam. "Emoticons." *Guardian,* 19 September 2002. Available online. URL: http://www.guardian.co.uk/news/2002/sep/19/netnotes. Accessed February 15, 2011. A history of the smiley language of emoticons.

WEB SITES

Emoticons. MSN Messenger. Available online. URL: http://messenger.msn.com/Resource/Emoticons.aspx. Accessed February 15, 2011. A chart showing emoticons, their meanings, and their keyboard equivalents.

Ethics in Computing. North Carolina State University. Available online. URL: http://ethics.csc.ncsu.edu/speech/netiquette. Accessed February 15, 2011. A comprehensive guide to online etiquette, with links to source documents such as Sally Hambridge's *Netiquette Guidelines—RFC1855.*

Net Etiquette. Albion Web site. Available online. URL: http://www.albion.com/netiquette/index.html. Accessed February 15, 2011. A guide to common courtesy online and the informal rules of cyberspace. Includes excerpts from Virginia Shea's *Netiquette.*

INDEX

Italic page numbers indicate illustrations.